Think Twice

Communication activities for beginner to intermediate students

David Hover

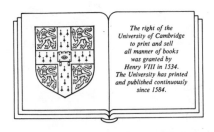

The right of the
University of Cambridge
to print and sell
all manner of books
was granted by
Henry VIII in 1534.
The University has printed
and published continuously
since 1584.

Cambridge University Press
Cambridge
London   New York   New Rochelle
Melbourne   Sydney

To Sylvine
and my grandmother

Published by the Press Syndicate of the University of Cambridge
The Pitt Building, Trumpington Street, Cambridge CB2 1RP
32 East 57th Street, New York, NY 10022, USA
10 Stamford Road, Oakleigh, Melbourne 3166, Australia

© Cambridge University Press 1986

First published 1986

Book designed and illustrated by Passim Ltd, Oxford

Printed in Great Britain at The Bath Press, Avon

ISBN 0 521 27385 4 Student's Book
ISBN 0 521 27386 2 Teacher's Book

CONTENTS

UNIT 1   personal identity (name, address, etc.); the alphabet; numbers

UNIT 2   *there is/are*; simple adjectives of places and people; *have (got)*; *can*; *like*

AUTHOR'S ACKNOWLEDGEMENTS

I would like to thank Rod Webb for the help and advice he gave in starting this book and contributing the basic ideas for activities 1, 2, 8, 13 and 16.

I would also like to thank Richard Cowan, Martin Dodman, Judith Port-Fox, Ruth Sacks, John Thompson, Andrew Wordsworth and the teachers at ECCIP, Paris, for all their advice and criticism at various stages of this book.

I join with the publishers in expressing my thanks and appreciation to the following institutions who tested the Pilot Edition: The British Centre, Venice, Italy; The British Institute, Barcelona, Spain; The British Institute of Rome, Italy; The British School, Florence, Italy; The English Language Centre, Hove, Brighton, England; Godmer House, Oxford, England; The International Language Centre, Tokyo, Japan; The Regent School, Rome, Italy; Volkshochschule, Frankfurt, West Germany; Women's Institute for Continuing Education, Paris, France; Weiterbildungkurs, Dubendorf, Switzerland.

ACKNOWLEDGEMENTS

The author and publishers are grateful to the following for permission to reproduce photographs and illustrations:

San Francisco Archives (apartment block in Activity 17); Ann Ronan Picture Library (illustration on p.52); Ewing Galloway (photographs in Activity 27); Popperfoto (photographs on pp. 73, 93 top, 94 middle and right, 95 bottom); Richard and Sally Greenhill (photographs on pp. 93 bottom left, 95 top); Robert Canault/VIVA (photograph on p.93 bottom right); Rex Features Ltd (photograph on p.94 bottom left); Barnaby's Picture Library (photographs on p.96 top and bottom left).

The photographs on p.17 were taken by David Hover; on pp. 21, 22 and 57 by Rhea Views; on p.24 by Chris Honeywell.

The photographs on pp. 18, 23, 25, 26, 29, 30, 33, 34, 43, 44, 58, 65, 66, 74, 79, 80, 81, 82, 83 and 84 were taken by Designers and Partners.

The illustrations were drawn by Barbara Cooper.
Artwork by Designers and Partners, Oxford.

TO THE STUDENT

(use your dictionary!)

Before the activity

Read the instructions *carefully*: Do you understand everything?
What exactly is the situation? Can you imagine it?
What do you have to do? What do you want to ask your partner?

Ask your teacher if you have any problems.

Don't start working with your partner until you're sure you're ready.

During the activity

Never look at your partner's page. If you don't understand, ask him to repeat or explain.

Don't ask your teacher for vocabulary or correction. If you don't know a word, find different words to explain it.

Say *everything* in English.

The activity isn't an exercise, so enjoy talking. Add your own comments. Improvise a little.

After the activity

What problems did you have? Was your English clear and accurate?
What should you work on or revise?

TO THE TEACHER

The activities in *Think Twice* put students in situations where they have to communicate with each other independently of you, the teacher.

The students work in pairs or small groups, and are given a problem to solve or a decision to make together. Each student has some, but not all the information needed to do this, so they have to ask each other for the information they haven't got. Each activity is self-sufficient and the students can be left to cope entirely on their own.

The language the students need for each activity is limited to one or two structures, so that once they are reasonably competent in those structures, you can introduce the activity as further practice. However, the students should not be made to feel that they are doing an exercise. The main point is to communicate effectively, even if that involves improvising language which is structurally incorrect.

The students' material includes letters, articles, etc., and in many of the activities the students are expected to scan these to find the information they need. The 'Introduction to scanning' on page 9 will help you to demonstrate this skill if your students are not already familiar with it.

The main objective of *Think Twice* is that, with continued use, it will help beginner and intermediate students to cope independently in the English-speaking world outside the classroom.

The organization of the book

- The activities are divided into units, with each unit based on a set of structures (see Contents). They are generally presented in order of difficulty, but each activity can be used independently of the others.
- The material for Student A is marked with one diagonal stripe in a top corner of the page concerned. The material for Student B, marked with two diagonal stripes, is on the following page.
- The Teacher's Book gives full notes regarding the language needed for each activity, ways of setting it up and exploiting it, alternative activities to practise the same structures, and ideas for follow-up discussions and homework.

Note: The student is referred to as 'he' or 'him' simply because the English pronoun system forces us to choose between 'he' and 'she'.

INTRODUCTION TO SCANNING

Read this letter.

Club Méditérranée
Tunisia

4th August

Dear Mum and Dad,

    Sit down before you read this, 'cos I've got the most amazing news! I'm engaged, yes, really, truly engaged to be married! Her name - my fiancée's name - is Sonia. It all happened in the bar at the Club. We just looked at each other and woosh! Love at first sight.

    She's Swedish, and she can't speak English very well, but it doesn't matter. She's a receptionist in Stockholm, you see, so she knows a few words and I'm teaching her the rest.

    I'm sure you'll take to her. I'm bringing her over to London at the end of the holiday to meet you before she goes back to Sweden. I've invited her parents over for Christmas too, and I think she understands, but it's hard to tell sometimes.

    Can you send £200 for a diamond ring? They're very expensive over here, but I want to buy one as soon as possible so that we can have an enormous party and make it official.

Lots and lots of love,

Tony

Answer these questions.

Who's the letter to?
Who's it from?
Where is he?
Is he married?

What's her name?
Where's she from?
What's her job?
Where does she live?

Can she speak English?
How much money does he want?
Why?

Is it difficult? Perhaps you're trying to read everything. Look at this.

Club Méditérranée
Tunisia

4th August

Dear Mum and Dad,

    Sit down before you read this, 'cos I've got the most amazing news! I'm engaged, yes, really, truly engaged to be married! Her name - my fiancée's name - is Sonia. It all happened in the bar at the Club. We just looked at each other and woosh! Love at first sight.

    She's Swedish, and she can't speak English very well, but it doesn't matter. She's a receptionist in Stockholm, you see, so she knows a few words and I'm teaching her the rest.

    I'm sure you'll take to her. I'm bringing her over to London at the end of the holiday to meet you before she goes back to Sweden. I've invited her parents over for Christmas too, and I think she understands, but it's hard to tell sometimes.

    Can you send £200 for a diamond ring? They're very expensive over here, but I want to buy one as soon as possible so that we can have an enormous party and make it official.

Lots and lots of love,

Tony

Can you answer the questions now?

SCANNING

Reading passage supplementary to Activity 13, pages 35 and 36

Alan lives in Spa. How do you get to his house
from the station?
Mark his house on your
maps.

36 Alma Street
Spa, Avon

Dear Anna,
It's lovely to hear you're coming after all. I'm afraid I won't be able to meet you at the station, as I'll be at work. There isn't a bus route that goes near the station either, so you'd better walk and leave your case at the station. It's not far, and I'll pick the case up later.

Anyway here's how you get to the house. Turn left outside the station and go down College Street. At the end of the street, turn right into Exchange Road. Go down Exchange Road (you'll cross Victoria Road and go past a church on your right). Then turn left at the Theatre Royal — I forget the name of the road. Anyway, Alma Street's the third street on the left. There's a phone box on the corner and a car park opposite, so it's easy to find. Number 36 is at the very end of the street, next to the river.

It'll be lovely to see you again. Ask the neighbours at 34 for a key.

Lots of love,
Alan

Reading passage supplementary to Activity 28, pages 69 and 70

jewel that is the island
wenty of us gathered
art nature expedition,
the vast assortment of
memory of one towers
is of the large Red
the nearby Seychelles
ooked with consumate
managed one of the
First one eye and then
alefully as the corres-
gonally slashed and
d seasoning on one
children present) and
addition of fiery green
and crammed into the
.t. Wrapped securely in
placed on the suitably
thirty five minutes, and
esults were staggering.
ing and eclectic book
reprinted by Penguin,
en praises the effect

Seminar at the Java Hotel

October 3rd
Speaker: **Mr John Appleby**

The seminar started at 5.30pm. First, Mr Appleby talked about newspapers in America for an hour and a half. After that he showed us some newspapers and we asked him questions.

We had dinner in the hotel restaurant at 7.30. After dinner we watched a short film (30 minutes) about making newspapers, and then there was a discussion about the film. The seminar finished at 10.30.

not, g
ss and black
good made as sma
useful with drinks or
smoked salmon a
ment on the origi
two of cream ligh
the filling.

All the dishes
accompanied be
salads, and perha
and pork with a f
split open, and do
chives. Unadultera
follow, with a spr
lops of clotted cr
bananas baked i
embers of the fire
the finishing touch
the ubiquitous eld
queen of summer

Elderflo

You and your partner

Who is he?

You and your partner

Who is he?

MS/352/6XF

West Sussex County Police
21/33 Randolph Street
Ryeport
West Sussex

MISSING PERSONS DECLARATION FORM

	First Name(s):
Surname:	Date of Birth:
Mr/Mrs/Miss/Ms	Marital Status:		Tel.
Address:			
Occupation:			

You are a secretary at the Social Security offices.

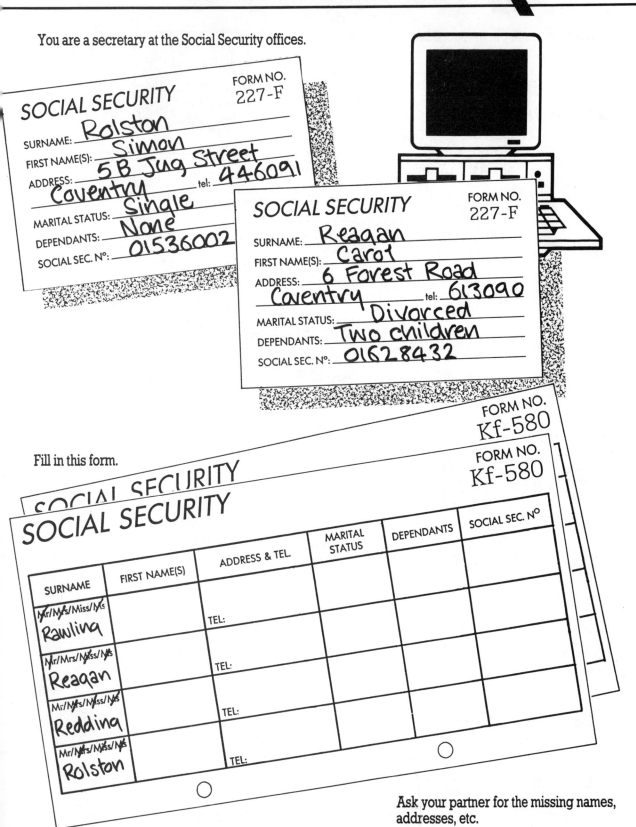

SOCIAL SECURITY FORM NO. 227-F

SURNAME: Rolston
FIRST NAME(S): Simon
ADDRESS: 5 B Jug Street
Coventry   tel: 446091
MARITAL STATUS: Single
DEPENDANTS: None
SOCIAL SEC. Nº: 01536002

SOCIAL SECURITY FORM NO. 227-F

SURNAME: Reagan
FIRST NAME(S): Carol
ADDRESS: 6 Forest Road
Coventry   tel: 613090
MARITAL STATUS: Divorced
DEPENDANTS: Two children
SOCIAL SEC. Nº: 01628432

Fill in this form.

SOCIAL SECURITY FORM NO. Kf-580

SURNAME	FIRST NAME(S)	ADDRESS & TEL.	MARITAL STATUS	DEPENDANTS	SOCIAL SEC. Nº
Mr/Mrs/Miss/Ms Rawling		TEL:			
Mr/Mrs/Miss/Ms Reagan		TEL:			
Mr/Mrs/Miss/Ms Redding		TEL:			
Mr/Mrs/Miss/Ms Rolston		TEL:			

Ask your partner for the missing names, addresses, etc.

You are a secretary at the Social Security offices.

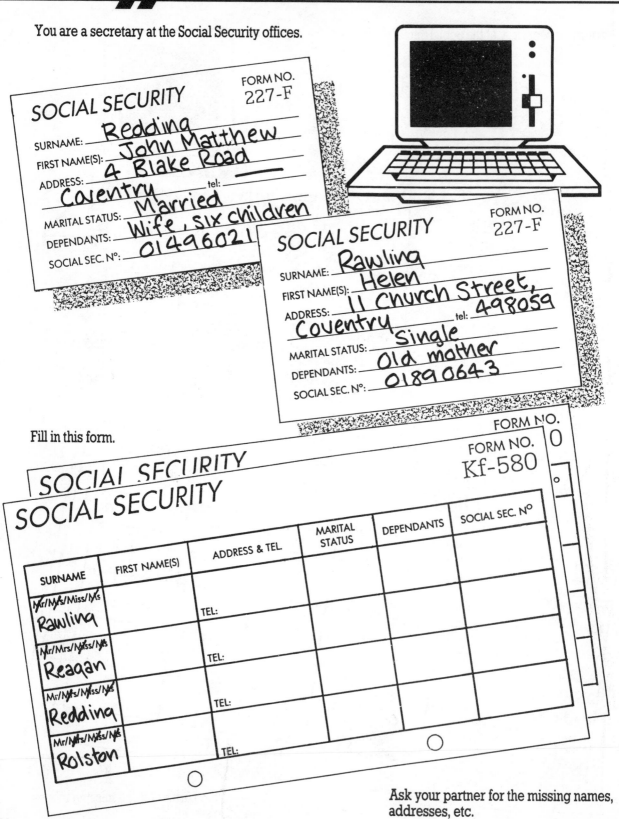

SOCIAL SECURITY FORM NO. 227-F

SURNAME: Redding
FIRST NAME(S): John Matthew
ADDRESS: 4 Blake Road
Coventry tel: —
MARITAL STATUS: Married
DEPENDANTS: Wife, six children
SOCIAL SEC. N°: 0149 6021

SOCIAL SECURITY FORM NO. 227-F

SURNAME: Rawling
FIRST NAME(S): Helen
ADDRESS: 11 Church Street, Coventry tel: 498059
MARITAL STATUS: Single
DEPENDANTS: Old mother
SOCIAL SEC. N°: 0189 0643

Fill in this form.

SOCIAL SECURITY FORM NO. Kf-580

SURNAME	FIRST NAME(S)	ADDRESS & TEL.	MARITAL STATUS	DEPENDANTS	SOCIAL SEC. N°
Mr/Mrs/Miss/Ms Rawling		TEL:			
Mr/Mrs/Miss/Ms Reagan		TEL:			
Mr/Mrs/Miss/Ms Redding		TEL:			
Mr/Mrs/Miss/Ms Rolston		TEL:			

Ask your partner for the missing names, addresses, etc.

At a reception.

THANK YOU.

HELLO. I'M CORINNE MILLS.

HERE'S MY CARD.

DAG RUDVIN
SJEFREDAKTØR/
MANAGING EDITOR

Norsk Forlag
St Olavs plass, Oslo 1
Tlf. (02) 20 07 10

NICE TO MEET YOU. I'M DAN SMITH, AND THIS IS... I'M SORRY, WHAT'S YOUR NAME AGAIN?

JUDITH BITTING.

After the reception.
You've got these cards ...

... but you haven't got the cards for these people.
Ask your partner about them.

SCHOOLS BOOKSTORE CO., LTD.

YONEZO SUZUKI
MANAGER
FOREIGN BOOKS DEPT

9 CHOME
CHUO-KU. TOKYO 103,
Tel: (03) 595 – 9332

Macdonald-Higgins

Bayomy Awad بيومي عوض
Editor مصرر

International Management
Macdonald-Higgins House
Maidenhead, Berkshire SL6 2QL, England.
Telephone: (0628) 64561   Telex: 743244

CHEMICO PLAN
CONTROL SYSTEMS LTD

JUDITH BITTING
ACCOUNTANT

88 Chester Court Mansions,
Chester Avenue,
London WC1B 3AE
Telephone: 01 – 680 6414   Telex: 880 753

—Corinne mills
   job? company?
   address? tel?

—Mr Paques (sales representative)
   first name?
   Company? tel?

—Anne Court
   job? company?

—The manager of Shop Photo
in Paris: name? address?

15

Aziz is on holiday. These are his photos.
Who's in the photos? Are they in Italy? Japan? . . .
Ask your partner, and write their names in the family tree.

Aziz = _____

This is part of a letter about your partner's photos.

I'm sending a couple of photos with this letter.
One photo is of Christ Church College in Oxford.
Carol, my mother (she's on the right), is with her
sister, Anne, and my brother, James. I'm in the
photo on the river Cherwell with Ron (my father).
       See you soon
          love,
             Karen

Karen is on holiday. These are her photos.
Who's in the photos? Are they in Italy? Japan? . . .
Ask your partner, and write their names in the family tree.

CHRIST

MEMBERS
ARE WE
CHI
IS
SECON
MEM

=

Karen

This is part of a letter about your partner's photos.

I thought you'd like to see a recent photo of them all.

One photograph is of me and my wife Sosan on a bridge in Paris. Photograph number two is of my daughter, Mumtaz (on the left) with my wife's friend Burkut, and my son Anwar at the Eiffel Tower.

love to you all
Aziz

Mrs Barnes

delivery man

3 TINS OF TUNA

1. You are the delivery man. Your partner is Mrs Barnes.

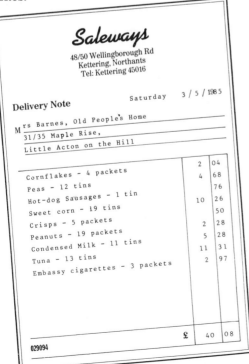

Saleways

48/50 Wellingborough Rd
Kettering, Northants
Tel: Kettering 45016

Delivery Note Saturday 3 / 5 / 1985

Mrs Barnes, Old People's Home
31/35 Maple Rise,
Little Acton on the Hill

Cornflakes - 4 packets	2	04
Peas - 12 tins	4	68
Hot-dog Sausages - 1 tin		76
Sweet corn - 19 tins	10	26
Crisps - 5 packets		50
Peanuts - 19 packets	2	28
Condensed Milk - 11 tins	5	28
Tuna - 13 tins	11	31
Embassy cigarettes - 3 packets	2	97
	£ 40	08

029094

2. You are Mrs Barnes. Your partner is the delivery man.

Shopping   (May 10th)

27 large tins of hot-dog sausages

13 medium tins of sweet corn

64 large tins of tuna

68 large packets of cornflakes

25 small packets of crisps

40 packets of Marlboro (cigarettes)

70 packets of Rothmans (cigarettes)

19 small packets of peanuts

30 small tins of condensed milk

80 large tins of peas

Mrs Barnes

delivery man

3 Tins of TUNA

1. You are Mrs Barnes. Your partner is the delivery man.

Shopping (May 3rd)

4 packets of cornflakes
20 tins of peas
1 tin of hot-dog sausages
9 tins of sweet corn
15 packets of crisps
19 packets of peanuts
11 tins of condensed milk
3 tins of tuna
3 packets of Embassy
        (cigarettes)

2. You are the delivery man. Your partner is Mrs Barnes.

Saleways

48/50 Wellingborough Rd
Kettering, Northants
Tel: Kettering 45016

Delivery Note   Saturday 10 / 5 / 19 85

Mrs Barnes, Old People's Home
31/35 Maple Rise,
Little Acton on the Hill

Cornflakes (large packets) 68		34	68
Condensed Milk (small tins) 30		14	40
Tuna (large tins) 46		40	02
Peanuts (small packets) 90		10	80
Hot-dog Sausages(large tins) 27		20	52
Peas (large tins) 18		7	02
Sweet Corn (medium tins) 30		16	20
Crisps (small packets) 25		2	50
Cigarettes: Marlboro 40		42	80
Rothmans 17		16	83

029210

£ 205 77

John is on holiday in Corsica, at the Piano Hotel.

CORSICA

PIANO HOTEL
★ ★

20 rooms with a shower, WC, telephone and balcony.
Restaurant, bar, television room, tennis court.
100 metres from a large beach.

2 kilometres from Valettio, a small town with a cinema,
restaurants and two supermarkets.

PRICES PER PERSON FROM LONDON (return)
for one week on full board:

26 March to 29 April	30 April to 29 July	30 July to 15 Sept.

This is a postcard from John.
  What's good about the holiday?
  What isn't good?

Dear Alex,
   I've had quite a good
holiday so far. The beach
is lovely and it isn't
crowded at all. As for the
food, the restaurant in the
hotel is very good, and the
supermarkets in the town
are cheap. But there isn't
a discotheque and the
restaurants in the town
are very expensive, so
evening life is a bit
boring. There isn't a
swimming pool at the
hotel, either.
   Still, the weather's great!
         Much love John

Alex Holland
28 Ealing Rd
London SW3 6BF
Angleterre

He wants to stay at a different hotel.

His friend, Carol, is at the Marina Hotel. Your
partner has got a brochure about the hotel and a
postcard from Carol.

Is the Marina Hotel right for John? Ask your
partner about it — Is there a swimming pool? Is
the beach crowded? etc.

Carol is on holiday in Corsica, at the Marina Hotel.

CORSICA

MARINA HOTEL
★ ★ ★

63 rooms with bath, WC, telephone and balcony. Restaurant, 3 bars, swimming pool, discotheque, ping-pong room, 2 tennis courts, 60 metres from the beach.

1 kilometre from Colvi, a village with 2 restaurants, small shops and a market.

PRICES PER PERSON FROM LONDON (return)
for one week on full board:

26 March to 29 April	30 April to 29 July	30 July to 15 Sept.

This is a postcard from Carol.
What's good about the holiday?
What isn't good?

Dear Martia,
   Guess what – a sad holiday postcard.
   I'm <u>not</u> happy here. The shops are expensive, the hotel and the beach are crowded (the beach is very small) and the discotheque is noisy. Fun, huh?!
   Its not all bad. The village is lovely – the restaurants are cheap and there's a good market for food and souvenirs. Oh yes, and the tennis courts at the hotel are very good. It's lovely playing in sunshine for once!
   lots of love,
   Carol

Martia Lawson
43 Riverside Ave,
London ·SW4 3AH
Angleterre

She wants to stay at a different hotel.

Her friend, John, is at the Piano Hotel. Your partner has got a brochure about the hotel and a postcard from John.

Is the Piano Hotel right for Carol? Ask your partner about it — Are the shops expensive? Is there a tennis court? etc.

These are photographs of models. Your partner is looking for a model for an advertisement. Is he looking for a man or a woman? young? romantic? sexy? . . .

Ask him, and then show him the right models.

Greg Ford

Corine White

Charles Forbes

Angela Howe

Sam Kaplan

Mary Livingstone

Henry Billing

Dorothy Short

John Pleasance

You're looking for a model for an advertisement for Clear Soap. Are you looking for a man or a woman? Young? romantic? sexy? . . .

Your partner has some photographs of models. Look at the photographs with him. Is the model *too* young? *too* romantic? . . .

You're also looking for a model (or models) for an advertisement for Marson's Tea.

Swop Shop is an agency for exchanges in London. Who can exchange?

Your partner has got seven different cards.

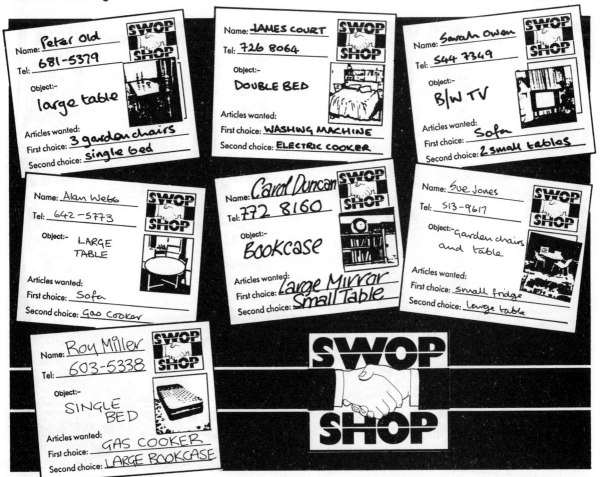

25

Swop Shop is an agency for exchanges in London. Your partner has got seven different cards.
Who can exchange?

Name: SAM BAKER
Tel: 643 — 7582
Object:— SOFA
Articles wanted:
First choice: COLOUR TV
Second choice: WASHING MACHINE

Name: Joan Palmer
Tel: 739 — 4602
Object:— Mirror (Large)
Articles wanted:
First choice: Small table
Second choice: Bookcase

Name: Tina Perry
Tel: 926 — 6023
Object:— LARGE FRIDGE
Articles wanted:
First choice: Sofa
Second choice: Colour TV

Name: Karen Mills
Tel: 531 — 6262
Object:— FRIDGE
Articles wanted:
First choice: LARGE TABLE
Second choice: SOFA

Name: Diane Smith
Tel: 603 · 4089
Object:— WASHING MACHINE
Articles wanted:
First choice: Garden Chairs
Second choice: Single bed

Name: STEVE EVANS
Tel: 893 — 0579
Object:— COLOUR TV
Articles wanted:
First choice: Fridge
Second choice: Electric Cooker

Name: Harry Brook
Tel: 422 — 6194
Object:— ELECTRIC COOKER
Articles wanted:
First choice: Double Bed
Second choice: 2 single beds

BURBRIDGE

This is a map of Burbridge. Which streets are one-way? Where can you park? (etc.)

Your map doesn't show all the traffic signs in Burbridge. The other signs are on your partner's map.

NO ENTRY

ONE-WAY

CAR PARK

NO PARKING

NO CARS
(Pedestrian Area)
(░░░ on the map)

NO LEFT TURN

NO RIGHT TURN

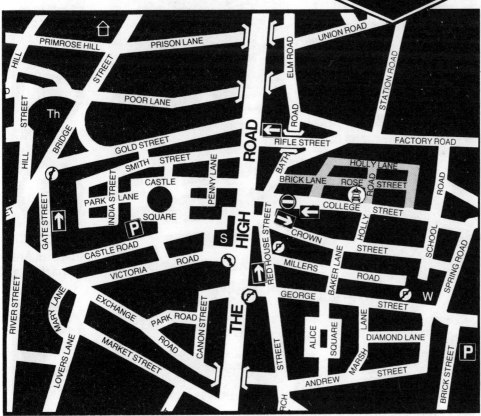

1. You are at work (W). You want to drive to the theatre (Th) and park near it. How can you go there? Ask your partner 'Can I . . . ?'

2. Your partner is at home (⌂). He wants to drive to the supermarket (S) and then to work (W). How can he go there? Where can he park?
(<u>Important</u>: When you are in Victoria Road you can't turn right into the High Road.)

NO ENTRY

ONE-WAY

CAR PARK

BURBRIDGE

This is a map of Burbridge. Which streets are one-way? Where can you park? (etc.)

Your map doesn't show all the traffic signs in Burbridge. The other signs are on your partner's map.

NO PARKING

NO CARS
(Pedestrian Area)
(on the map)

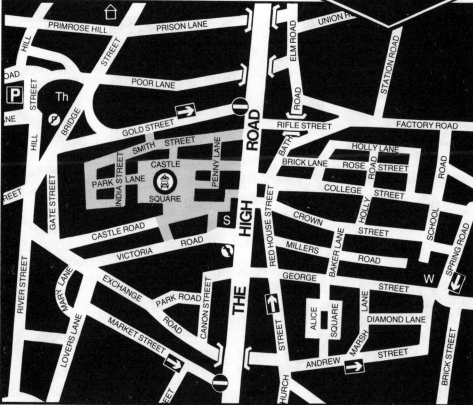

NO LEFT TURN

1. Your partner is at work (W). He wants to drive to the theatre (Th). How can he go there?
(<u>Important</u>: There's an accident in Exchange Road, between Victoria Road and Park Road.)

2. You are at home ( ). You want to drive to the supermarket (S) and park near it. Then you want to drive to work (W) and park your car. Ask your partner 'Can I . . .?'

NO RIGHT TURN

LOVE-MATCH 10A

The Love-Match Agency helps you to find friends.

Anne Kato is looking for a boy-friend. Fill in the form for her.

205 Union Road
London N.12
10th June

Dear Sir,

Here are the details you asked for in your letter of 24th May.

I'm 28 and single. My father is Japanese and my mother is English. I can speak a little Japanese, but not much, since my family left Japan when I was 6. I can speak French very well, though. Both come in very useful in my job - I'm a receptionist in a hotel - but since I can't drive and I don't like travelling at all, I don't use them much outside work.

As for sports, I can play tennis and I can dance very well. I like going out to discotheques very much.

I like staying in sometimes, but I can't cook so it usually depends on how hungry I am! At home I like reading and listening to records.

Yours sincerely,

Anne Kato

LOVE-MATCH AGENCY

NAME: _____
AGE: _____
JOB: _____

ABILITIES

sports: _____
foreign languages: _____
other (eg, driving, musical instrument): _____

LIKES

going out: _____

staying in: _____

other: _____

Is Bernado Travani the right boy-friend for Anne Kato? Can he do the same things?
Does he like the same things?
If he can't (or doesn't), does it matter?

LOVE-MATCH AGENCY

NAME: Bernardo Travani
AGE: 27
JOB: Journalist

ABILITIES

sports: Can play tennis (very well), ping-pong, dance
foreign languages: Spanish (very well), a little German
other (eg, driving, musical instrument): can drive, can draw very well

LIKES

going out: very much - likes going to the cinema and parties
staying in: very much
other: doesn't like cooking, likes travelling

LOVE-MATCH AGENCY

NAME: Hanna Buchner
AGE: 31
JOB: teacher

ABILITIES

sports: can play tennis and ping-pong (very well)
foreign languages: German
other (eg, driving, musical instrument): can drive very well, can play the piano

LIKES

going out: very much - likes going to restaurants (doesn't like dancing)
staying in: sometimes
other: travelling (very much) going to the theatre

Your partner has the form for George Shipway. Is he the right boy-friend for Anne?

29

The Love-Match Agency helps you to find friends. Housnu Kemal is looking for a girl-friend. Fill in the form for him.

18, Bath Street
London S.W.8

12th June 1985

Dear Sir,

In reply to your letter of 18th May, I'm 32 and divorced, but without any children. I can speak Arabic very well, and a little German. I like travelling very much, so I find the languages useful.

In my free time, I like going out sometimes - it depends what for. I don't like going to the cinema or discotheques, for example. I like dancing if the music is arabic.

I can play tennis and ping-pong very well and I like driving sports cars - I've got a 1967 Spitfire.

I like staying in very much. I can cook very well and I often invite my colleagues (I work in a bank) to dinner.

Yours sincerely,

Housnu Kemal

♥♥ LOVE-MATCH AGENCY

NAME: _____
AGE: _____
JOB: _____

ABILITIES
sports: _____
foreign languages: _____
other (eg, driving, musical instrument): _____
_____
_____

LIKES
going out: _____
_____
staying in: _____
_____
other: _____
_____

Is Bibi Daud the right girl-friend for Housnu Kemal? Can she do the same things? Does she like the same things?
If she can't (or doesn't), does it matter?

♥♥ LOVE-MATCH AGENCY

NAME: Bibi Daud
AGE: 29
JOB: taxi driver

ABILITIES
sports: can dance (very well)
foreign languages: a little French and a little Spanish
other (eg. driving, musical instrument): can drive, can draw

LIKES
going out: Sometimes - doesn't like going to the cinema or discos
staying in: very much
other: likes going for walks, doesn't like travelling

♥♥ LOVE-MATCH AGENCY

NAME: George Shipway
AGE: 35
JOB: Salesman

ABILITIES
sports: _____
foreign languages: French
other (eg. driving, musical instrument): can drive, can play the guitar a little

LIKES
going out: sometimes - doesn't like dancing
staying in: sometimes
other: likes reading

Your partner has the form for Hanna Buchner. Is she the right girl-friend for Housnu?

Are you the right weight? (+2kg or −2kg is OK.) If not, are you overweight or underweight?

Is your partner the right weight? Ask him the questions.

ARE YOU THE RIGHT WEIGHT?

MEN

Height	Weight		
	Small build	Medium build	Large build
154cm	52kg	55kg	60kg
157	54	57	62
160	55	59	63
163	57	61	65
166	59	63	67
169	61	65	70
172	63	67	72
175	65	70	74
178	67	72	76
181	70	74	79
184	72	76	82
187	74	79	84
190	76	81	87

WOMEN

Height	Weight		
	Small build	Medium build	Large build
142cm	42kg	46kg	50kg
145	43	47	51
148	45	49	53
151	47	50	55
154	48	52	57
157	50	54	59
160	52	56	61
163	54	58	63
166	56	60	65
169	58	62	67
172	60	64	69
175	62	66	72
178	65	68	74

THIS is the right weight if you're 25 years old.
If you're between 25 and 45, add half a kilogram per year (i.e. if you're 26 add ½kg, if you're 27 add 1kg, if you're 28 add 1½kg, etc.).
If you're over 45, add 10 kilograms.
If you're under 25, subtract half a kilogram per year.

You are at lunch with your partner in the Elmtree Restaurant. What would you like to eat?

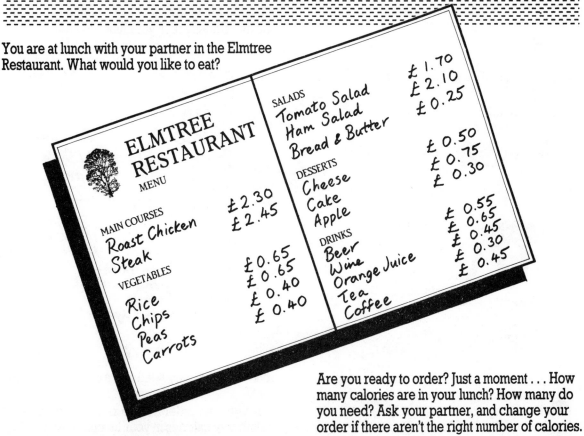

ELMTREE RESTAURANT

MENU

MAIN COURSES

Roast Chicken £2.30
Steak £2.45

VEGETABLES

Rice £0.65
Chips £0.65
Peas £0.40
Carrots £0.40

SALADS

Tomato Salad £1.70
Ham Salad £2.10
Bread & Butter £0.25

DESSERTS

Cheese £0.50
Cake £0.75
Apple £0.30

DRINKS

Beer £0.55
Wine £0.65
Orange Juice £0.45
Tea £0.30
Coffee £0.45

Are you ready to order? Just a moment ... How many calories are in your lunch? How many do you need? Ask your partner, and change your order if there aren't the right number of calories.

Are you the right weight? Answer your partner's questions.

You are at lunch with your partner in the Elmtree Restaurant. What would you like to eat?

ELMTREE RESTAURANT
MENU

MAIN COURSES

Roast Chicken	£2.30
Steak	£2.45

VEGETABLES

Rice	£0.65
Chips	£0.65
Peas	£0.40
Carrots	£0.40

SALADS

Tomato Salad	£1.70
Ham Salad	£2.10
Bread & Butter	£0.25

DESSERTS

Cheese	£0.50
Cake	£0.75
Apple	£0.30

DRINKS

Beer	£0.55
Wine	£0.65
Orange Juice	£0.45
Tea	£0.30
Coffee	£0.45

Are you ready to order? Just a moment . . . How many calories are in your lunch?

For weight watchers, this is a list of the **CALORIES IN TODAY'S MENU**

MAIN COURSES

Roast Chicken	225 cal
Steak	585 cal

VEGETABLES

Rice	600 cal
Chips	280 cal
Peas	55 cal
Carrots	20 cal

SALADS

Tomato Salad	70 cal
Ham Salad	140 cal

Bread	65 cal
Butter	100 cal

DESSERTS

Cheese	220 cal
Cake	115 cal
Apple	85 cal

DRINKS

Beer	180 cal
Wine	100 cal
Orange Juice	140 cal
Tea – 5. with milk – 15	
with sugar – 40	
Coffee – 5 white – 25	
with sugar – 50	

If they are the right weight, a woman needs about 650 calories at lunch, and a man needs about 900 calories. If they are overweight, they need less calories (under 650 or 900). If they are underweight, they need *more* calories (over 650 or 900).

Change your order if there aren't the right number of calories in your lunch.

You want to make a pizza. This is the recipe.

PIZZA

PIZZA WITH
HAM AND MUSHROOMS

(serves 4–6 people)

500g flour
1 teaspoon salt
2 teaspoons sugar
3 teaspoons yeast
2 eggs
a little oil
8 tomatoes
2 onions
150g mushrooms
250g cheese
12 black olives
100g ham

First put 1 ½ litres of warm water in a bowl. Mix with the sugar and then add the yeast. Leave the mixture for 10–15 minutes until

These things are in your kitchen. Have your got everything? What do you need?

FLOUR
200g

CHEESE
250g

MUSHROOMS
200g

1 LITRE
OIL

1 Kg

SUGAR

ENGLISH
MUSTARD

Has your partner got the other things you need?

You want to make a salad. This is the recipe.

SALAD

CHEESE AND TUNA SALAD

(serves 4–6 people)

1 lettuce
250g tuna
5 tomatoes
4 potatoes
200g ham
3 onions
3 eggs
100g cheese
6 tablespoons oil
2 tablespoons vinegar
1 tablespoon mustard

Wash the potatoes and put them in a saucepan with a little salt. Pour boiling water over them, until it comes about halfway up the pan, put on a tight lid and leave until they're cooked but still...

These things are in your kitchen. Have you got everything? What do you need?

Has your partner got the other things you need?

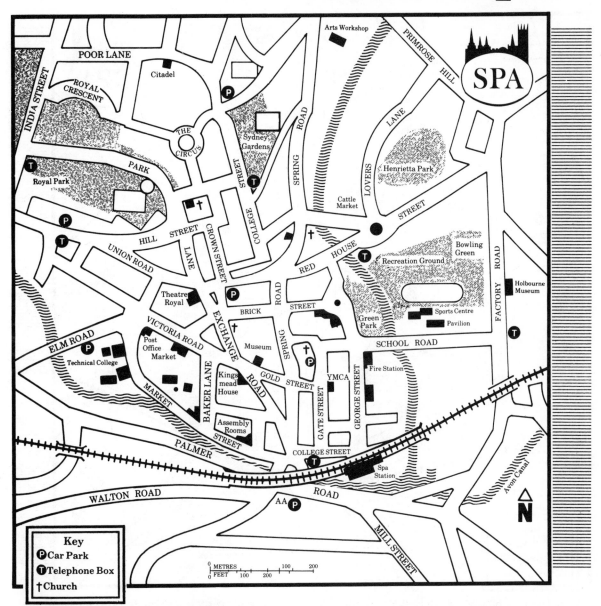

This is a plan of Spa, a town in England. Your partner is at the Holbourne Museum. He wants to go to the Technical College. This is the best route.

ROUTE

- ○ **HOLBOURNE MUSEUM**
- ● Sports Centre (School Road)
- ● All Saints Church (Gate Street)
- ● Gold Street
- ● Market (Victoria Road)
- ○ **MARKET STREET**

Practise the directions with the street names only. Then practise the directions with landmarks only (churches, telephone boxes, museums, etc.). Then give the directions to your partner with street names *and* landmarks.

You are at Spa Station. You want to go to the tennis courts. Ask your partner for directions.

(NB: See Reading Passage on Page 10.)

TEACHER'S NOTE: The students will come up against some surprises. Don't let them look at each other's material. They should cope in English.

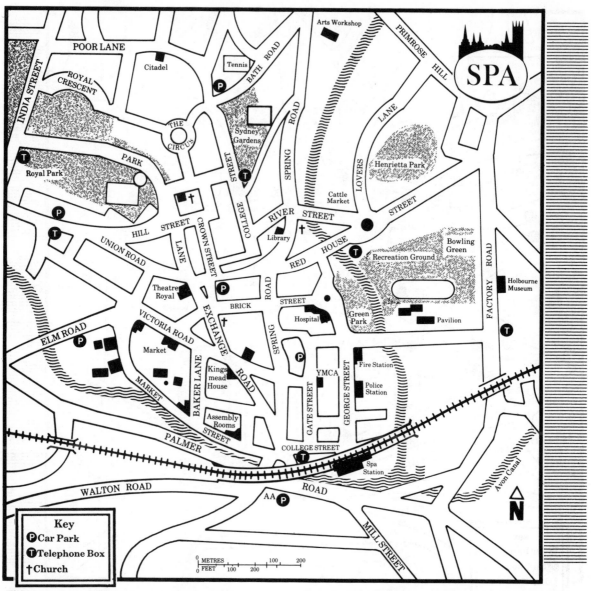

This is a plan of Spa, a town in England. Your partner is at Spa Station. He wants to go to the tennis courts. This is the best route.

ROUTE

○ **SPA STATION**
● Police Station (George Street)
● Hospital
● Spring Road
● River Street
● Sydney Gardens (College Street)
○ **BATH ROAD**

Practise the directions with the street names only. Then practise the directions with landmarks only (churches, telephone boxes, museums, etc.). Then give the directions to your partner with street names *and* landmarks.

You are at the Holbourne Museum. You want to go to the Technical College. Ask your partner for directions.

(NB: See Reading Passage on page 10.)

TEACHER'S NOTE: The students will come up against some surprises. Don't let them look at each other's material. They should cope in English.

You and your partner work in the theatre. You are directing a new play, *Fire and the Waters*. These are the instructions ('stage directions' in the theatre) for Act 1, Scene 1.

ACT 1   Scene 1

February, 1974. The scene opens on the Water's bedsit in Ealing. The room is spacious and Georgian, but the furniture has been assembled randomly from auctions and winter sales, resulting in what could almost be called style by its sheer eccentricity.

A heavy, round wooden table is next to the window (DSR) with three chairs around it. Two chairs are uncomfortably hard, but the third chair is low and soft with a towel draped over the back. Behind the table is a large double bed, piled high with various junk moved there to clear the main table. Between the bed and the door (USC) is a heavy wardrobe with a flimsy catch, which Roger Waters has improvised in the absence of the original.

Next to the bookcase (DSL) is the television with a sofa and an armchair in front of it. The sofa is small and uncomfortable, and clashes fairly violently with the large, soft armchair. A round carpet is in the centre of the room.

As the curtains open we find Elaine Waters hoovering the floor.

The stage directions are different for Act 2, Scene 3.
Ask your partner about them, and draw the furniture ('props' in the theatre) for Act 2, Scene 3 on the plan.

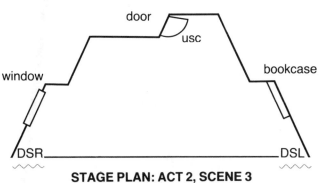

STAGE PLAN: ACT 2, SCENE 3

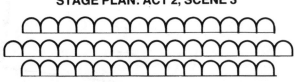

Props List   Act 2 Scene 3

bed
Wardrobe
TV
sofa
armchair
table
chairs
carpet
cushions.

What are the props like? Is the table, for example, round or square? large or small?

You and your partner work in the theatre. You are directing a new play, *Fire and the Waters*. These are the instructions ('stage directions' in the theatre) for Act 2, Scene 3.

ACT 2   Scene 3

May, 1974, evening. The room has changed considerably since the fire. It has been completely redecorated, leaving not a trace of the blackened debris from the previous act.

A new double bed is now next to the bookcase (DSL). It has been stripped of its sheets, which have been dumped near the door. Opposite the door is a small, light wardrobe with magazines, jumpers and other bric-a-brac already starting to pile up on it.

A small, colour TV is next to the window (DSR) with a long, low, comfortable sofa and two armchairs (also low and comfortable) in front of it. The room has obviously only just been vacated as there is a cigarette still burning in an ashtray on the floor next to the sofa.

A large, square table with two or three hard chairs is now behind the sofa and the armchair, and between the door and the window. In the centre of the room are three or four large cushions.

As the curtains open we hear an unfamiliar voice in the garden.

The stage directions are different for Act 1, Scene 1.
Ask your partner about them, and draw the furniture ('props' in the theatre) for Act 1, Scene 1 on the plan.

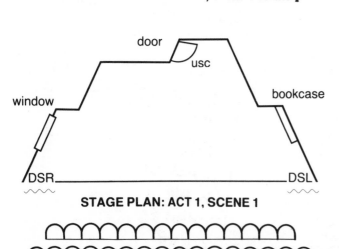

STAGE PLAN: ACT 1, SCENE 1

Props List   Act 1 Scene 1

TABLE
CHAIRS
BED
WARDROBE
T·V
SOFA
CUSHIONS
ARMCHAIR
CARPET.

What are the props like? Is the table, for example, round or square? large or small?

This is the BBC weather forecast for the United Kingdom today. Is it right? Your partner has the ITV weather forecast. Does he agree? If not, who is right? You or your partner?

Your partner also has the weather forecast in a newspaper, *The Daily Echo*. Does it agree with you or your partner?

When two weather forecasts agree for one of the towns, mark the weather next to that town on your map.

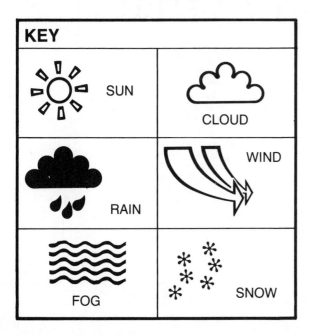

KEY

SUN	CLOUD
RAIN	WIND
FOG	SNOW

This is the ITV weather forecast for the United Kingdom today. Is it right? Your partner has the BBC weather forecast. Does he agree? If not, who is right? You or your partner?

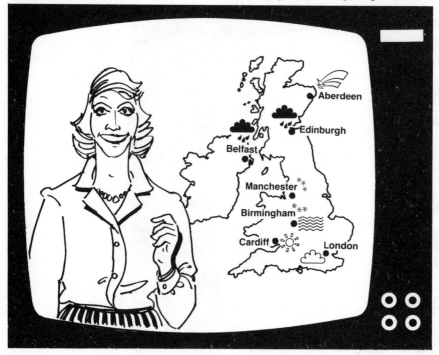

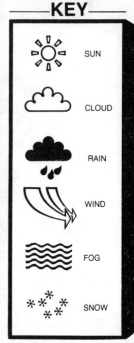

KEY

SUN	
CLOUD	
RAIN	
WIND	
FOG	
SNOW	

This is the weather forecast in *The Daily Echo*. Does it agree with you or your partner?

When two weather forecasts agree for one of the towns, it's probably the right weather for the town, so correct your ITV map.

TODAY'S WEATHER

The weather has been behaving very curiously these days. Extreme differences in conditions can be found within a few miles of each other. For example, it's snowing in Aberdeen, but a few miles south, in Edinburgh, it's beautifully sunny. According to Paul Alenby, our reporter in Edinburgh, this has meant that the hotels in Edinburgh are full of holiday makers from Aberdeen while the hotels in Aberdeen are full of (you guessed it!) skiers from Edinburgh.

Further south, around Manchester, it's cloudy and cold, but even that's better than Birming-ham, where it's snowing and very foggy. Birminghamites had better start copying the Scots in Aberdeen and leave for . . . Cardiff! In Cardiff it's hot and sunny almost like the South of France!

There are no surprises in London – it's raining, as always. Northern Ireland is generally warm for this time of year except for Belfast, where it's very windy due to a strong wind coming down off the North Sea.

Well, that's it for the weather today. Something for everyone, if you're close enough to get there. Happy driving!

You are on holiday in Farnmouth at Mrs Lowe's guest house.

It's Sunday, the last day of your holiday. (Your train leaves at 9.45 on Monday morning.)

Plan your day. (Your partner has got information about shops and the museum.)

Sunday 27 Last Day!

I want to:
- see 'What a Wallop!'
- buy food for lunch
- go to the beach (bus from Green Park)
- visit the museum

Sunday 27

Morning

Afternoon

Evening

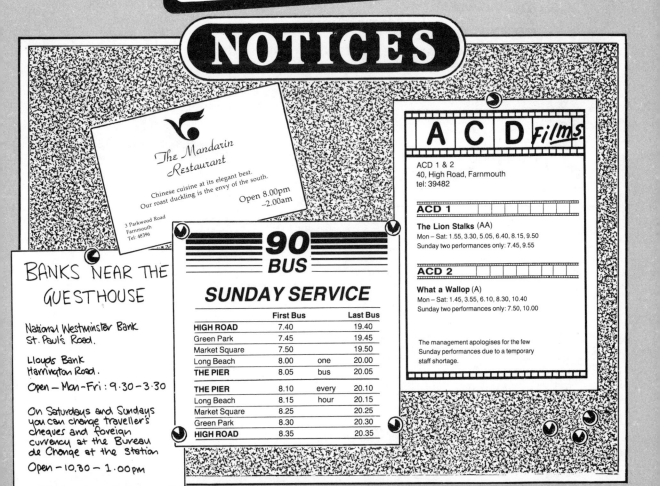

NOTICES

The Mandarin Restaurant

Chinese cuisine at its elegant best.
Our roast duckling is the envy of the south.

Open 8.00pm –2.00am

3 Parkwood Road
Farnmouth
Tel: 48396

ACD Films

ACD 1 & 2
40, High Road, Farnmouth
tel: 39482

ACD 1

The Lion Stalks (AA)
Mon – Sat: 1.55, 3.30, 5.05, 6.40, 8.15, 9.50
Sunday two performances only: 7.45, 9.55

ACD 2

What a Wallop (A)
Mon – Sat: 1.45, 3.55, 6.10, 8.30, 10.40
Sunday two performances only: 7.50, 10.00

The management apologises for the few Sunday performances due to a temporary staff shortage.

90 BUS

SUNDAY SERVICE

	First Bus		Last Bus
HIGH ROAD	7.40		19.40
Green Park	7.45		19.45
Market Square	7.50		19.50
Long Beach	8.00	one	20.00
THE PIER	8.05	bus	20.05
THE PIER	8.10	every	20.10
Long Beach	8.15	hour	20.15
Market Square	8.25		20.25
Green Park	8.30		20.30
HIGH ROAD	8.35		20.35

BANKS NEAR THE GUESTHOUSE

National Westminster Bank
St. Paul's Road.

Lloyds Bank
Harrington Road.
Open – Mon-Fri : 9·30 – 3·30

On Saturdays and Sundays you can change traveller's cheques and foreign currency at the Bureau de Change at the station

Open – 10.30 – 1·00pm

Your partner wants to do different things. Plan your day *together*.

You are on holiday in Farnmouth at Mrs Lowe's guest house.

It's Sunday, the last day of your holiday. (Your train leaves at 9.45 on Monday morning.)

Plan your day. (Your partner has got information about banks and a Chinese restaurant.)

Sunday 27 *Last Day*

I Want to:
- *go to the concert*
- *eat at a Chinese restaurant in the evening*
- *go to a disco*
- *No Money. change traveller's cheques*

Sunday 27

Morning

Afternoon

Evening

The one and only
PHIL HAYWORTH
and his magnificent
JAZZ BAND

Open-Air CONCERT in GREEN PARK

Every Sunday
from 1.30 pm to 2.30 pm

Admission:
adults £1.20   children 80p

Museum of Local Folklore and Customs

12 Madeira Road
(town centre)

Contains a rare and interesting collection of objects, prints and paintings of traditional life over the past 1000 years.

Opening times:
Mon – Sat 10a.m. – 5p.m.
Sundays 11a.m. – 3p.m.

MARY LOWE'S
GUEST HOUSE

Dear Guests,

I hope my little notice board keeps you well informed about everything in Farnmouth. Here are one or two extra items of information.

There's a market in the town centre every Saturday from 9 a.m. to 3 p.m.

I can recommend St Paul's as a very friendly church. On Sundays, morning service is from 10.30 to 11.30.

There's a supermarket (Allans) further up Landsdown Road. It's very useful because it stays open late on Friday evenings (until 8.00 p.m.) and it also opens on Sundays from 9.30 a.m. to 12.30 p.m.

Finally, there are two discotheques close to the guest house. Sloopy's Disco in Richardson Street opens at 8 p.m. and closes at 12.30 a.m. The Cavern in Florence Road opens at 10 p.m. and closes at about 5 a.m.

I hope you enjoy your stay.

Mary Lowe

Your partner wants to do different things. Plan your day *together*.

Mr and Mrs Brown and Mr and Mrs Johnson live in San Francisco. The Johnson family lives in the apartment above Mr and Mrs Brown.

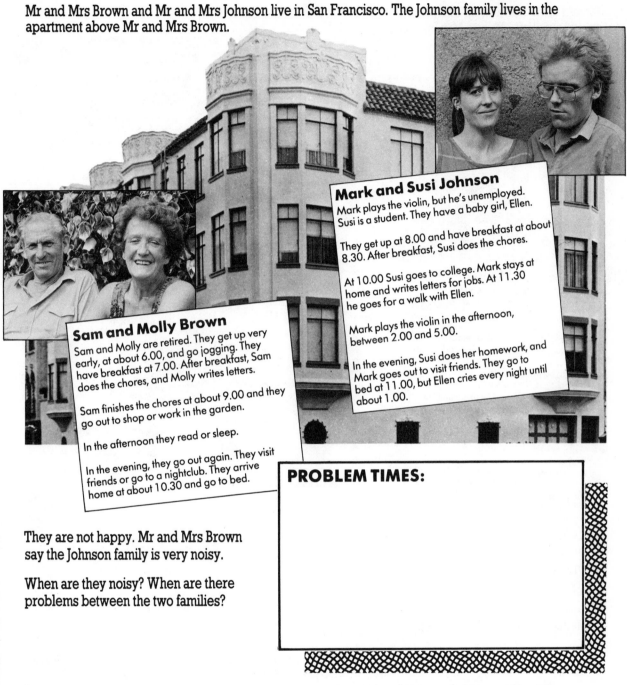

Mark and Susi Johnson

Mark plays the violin, but he's unemployed. Susi is a student. They have a baby girl, Ellen.

They get up at 8.00 and have breakfast at about 8.30. After breakfast, Susi does the chores.

At 10.00 Susi goes to college. Mark stays at home and writes letters for jobs. At 11.30 he goes for a walk with Ellen.

Mark plays the violin in the afternoon, between 2.00 and 5.00.

In the evening, Susi does her homework, and Mark goes out to visit friends. They go to bed at 11.00, but Ellen cries every night until about 1.00.

Sam and Molly Brown

Sam and Molly are retired. They get up very early, at about 6.00, and go jogging. They have breakfast at 7.00. After breakfast, Sam does the chores, and Molly writes letters.

Sam finishes the chores at about 9.00 and they go out to shop or work in the garden.

In the afternoon they read or sleep.

In the evening, they go out again. They visit friends or go to a nightclub. They arrive home at about 10.30 and go to bed.

PROBLEM TIMES:

They are not happy. Mr and Mrs Brown say the Johnson family is very noisy.

When are they noisy? When are there problems between the two families?

Your partner knows two other families in the building, Mr and Mrs Ketcham and Mr and Mrs Allen. They've got problems too!

The four families can exchange apartments (all the apartments in the building are the same). Ask your partner about his two families. What time do they get up? What do they do in the morning? afternoon? etc.

Who can live with Mr and Mrs Brown? Who can live with the Johnson family?

Mr and Mrs Allen and Mr and Mrs Ketcham live in San Francisco. The Allen family lives in the apartment above Mr and Mrs Ketcham.

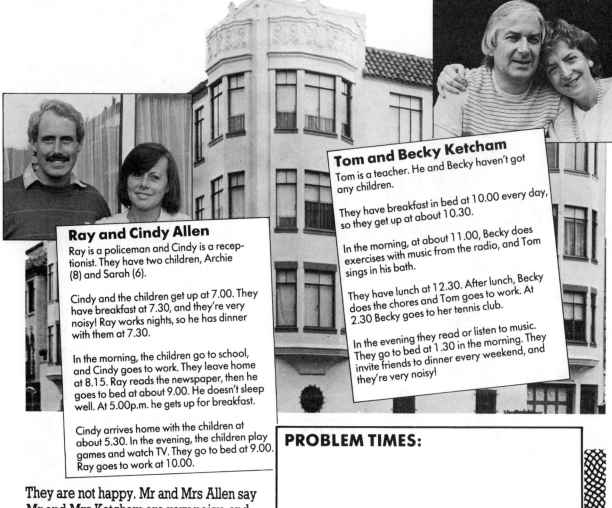

Tom and Becky Ketcham

Tom is a teacher. He and Becky haven't got any children.

They have breakfast in bed at 10.00 every day, so they get up at about 10.30.

In the morning, at about 11.00, Becky does exercises with music from the radio, and Tom sings in his bath.

They have lunch at 12.30. After lunch, Becky does the chores and Tom goes to work. At 2.30 Becky goes to her tennis club.

In the evening they read or listen to music. They go to bed at 1.30 in the morning. They invite friends to dinner every weekend, and they're very noisy!

Ray and Cindy Allen

Ray is a policeman and Cindy is a receptionist. They have two children, Archie (8) and Sarah (6).

Cindy and the children get up at 7.00. They have breakfast at 7.30, and they're very noisy! Ray works nights, so he has dinner with them at 7.30.

In the morning, the children go to school, and Cindy goes to work. They leave home at 8.15. Ray reads the newspaper, then he goes to bed at about 9.00. He doesn't sleep well. At 5.00p.m. he gets up for breakfast.

Cindy arrives home with the children at about 5.30. In the evening, the children play games and watch TV. They go to bed at 9.00. Ray goes to work at 10.00.

PROBLEM TIMES:

They are not happy. Mr and Mrs Allen say Mr and Mrs Ketcham are very noisy, and Mr and Mrs Ketcham say the Allen family is very noisy!

When are they noisy? When are there problems between the two families?

Your partner knows two other families in the building, Mr and Mrs Brown and Mr and Mrs Johnson. They've got problems too!

The four families can exchange apartments (all the apartments in the building are the same). Ask your partner about his two families. What time do they get up? What do they do in the morning? afternoon? etc.

Who can live with Mr and Mrs Ketcham? Who can live with the Allen family?

THE HOUSING COMMITTEE 18A

You and your partner work for the City Council in Cambourne, Australia. You are on the Housing Committee. The Housing Committee helps people to find flats and houses.

Anne Littleton and Harry Marden are looking for flats. The information about them is in the letters and the notes. Answer your partner's questions so he can fill in the forms for them.

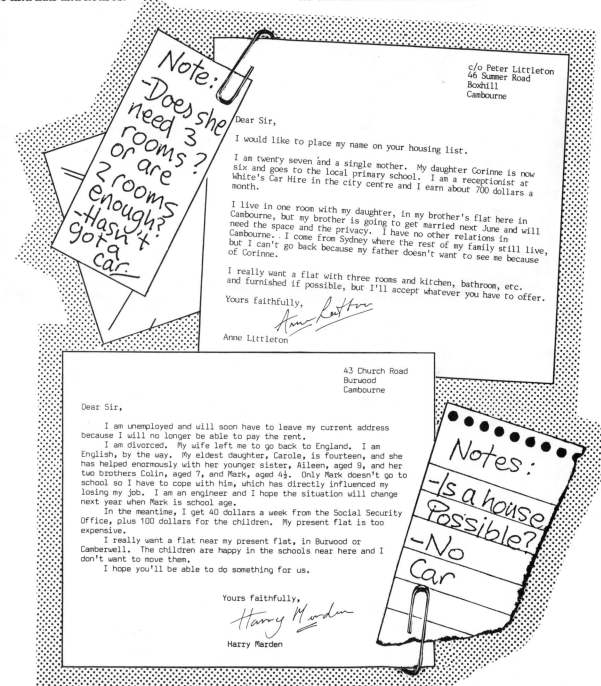

> **Note:**
> - Does she need 3 rooms? or are 2 rooms enough?
> - Hasn't got a car.

c/o Peter Littleton
46 Summer Road
Boxhill
Cambourne

Dear Sir,

I would like to place my name on your housing list.

I am twenty seven and a single mother. My daughter Corinne is now six and goes to the local primary school. I am a receptionist at White's Car Hire in the city centre and I earn about 700 dollars a month.

I live in one room with my daughter, in my brother's flat here in Cambourne, but my brother is going to get married next June and will need the space and the privacy. I have no other relations in Cambourne. I come from Sydney where the rest of my family still live, but I can't go back because my father doesn't want to see me because of Corinne.

I really want a flat with three rooms and kitchen, bathroom, etc. and furnished if possible, but I'll accept whatever you have to offer.

Yours faithfully,

Anne Littleton

43 Church Road
Burwood
Cambourne

Dear Sir,

I am unemployed and will soon have to leave my current address because I will no longer be able to pay the rent.

I am divorced. My wife left me to go back to England. I am English, by the way. My eldest daughter, Carole, is fourteen, and she has helped enormously with her younger sister, Aileen, aged 9, and her two brothers Colin, aged 7, and Mark, aged 4½. Only Mark doesn't go to school so I have to cope with him, which has directly influenced my losing my job. I am an engineer and I hope the situation will change next year when Mark is school age.

In the meantime, I get 40 dollars a week from the Social Security Office, plus 100 dollars for the children. My present flat is too expensive.

I really want a flat near my present flat, in Burwood or Camberwell. The children are happy in the schools near here and I don't want to move them.

I hope you'll be able to do something for us.

Yours faithfully,

Harry Marden

> **Notes:**
> - Is a house possible?
> - No car

Now look at the houses and flats on page 48. Decide with your partner: Which flat (or house) can you give to Anne Littleton? Harry Marden? What do they *need*?

45

Yuon Hou is looking for a flat. Fill in the form for him.

c/o Phnom Penh Stores
43 Cork Place
Cambourne

Dear Sir

Our home has been destroyed by fire and I do not know where I can turn. My wife, her aunt and our two small children now sleep on the floor of a friend's shop while I sleep in my taxi.

We can pay a fair rent. As you see, I am a taxi driver and I earn 600 dollars a month on average. My wife works three days a week in my friend's shop and earns about 200 dollars a month for this. Ngoc, my eldest son, is seven years old and goes to school. Minh, my other son, is only three and a half years old, so he doesn't go to school yet. My wife's aunt doesn't work because she is too old.

We would like an unfurnished flat. We come from Cambodia, so we like Cambodian furniture, and friends will help us to find that.

Thank you for your interest.

Yours faithfully

Yuon Hou

Yuon Hou

Notes:
- aunt has problems with her back. Needs ground or 1st floor flat?

HSB 165

CAMBOURNE CITY COUNCIL
HOUSING COMMITTEE

HOUSING REQUEST FORM

		age
	first name(s)	
	marital status	
surname	address	
mr/mrs/miss/ms		
nationality	place of work	
	other salaries/income	
profession		occupation
salary	age	
dependants		
accommodation wanted		

Now look at the houses and flats on page 48. Which flat (or house) can you give to him?

You and your partner work for the City Council in Cambourne, Australia. You are on the Housing Committee. The Housing Committee helps people to find flats or houses.

Anne Littleton and Harry Marden are looking for flats. Your partner has got letters from them with notes. Ask him about them and fill in the forms.

RECEIVED

CAMBOURNE CITY COUNCIL
HOUSING COMMITTEE

HSB 165

HOUSING REQUEST FORM

surname	first name(s)	
mr/mrs/miss/ms	marital status	age
nationality	address	

profession	place of work	
salary	other salaries/income	
dependants	age	occupation

accommodation wanted

CAMBOURNE CITY COUNCIL
HOUSING COMMITTEE

HSB 165

HOUSING REQUEST FORM

surname	first name(s)	
mr/mrs/miss/ms	marital status	age
nationality	address	

profession	place of work	
salary	other salaries/income	
dependants	age	occupation

accommodation wanted

Now look at the houses and flats on page 48 with your partner. Decide together: Which flat (or house) can you give to Anne Littleton? Harry Marden? What do they *need?*

Which flat (or house) can you give to Yuon Hou? Anne Littleton? Harry Marden? What exactly do they *need*? Decide with your partner.

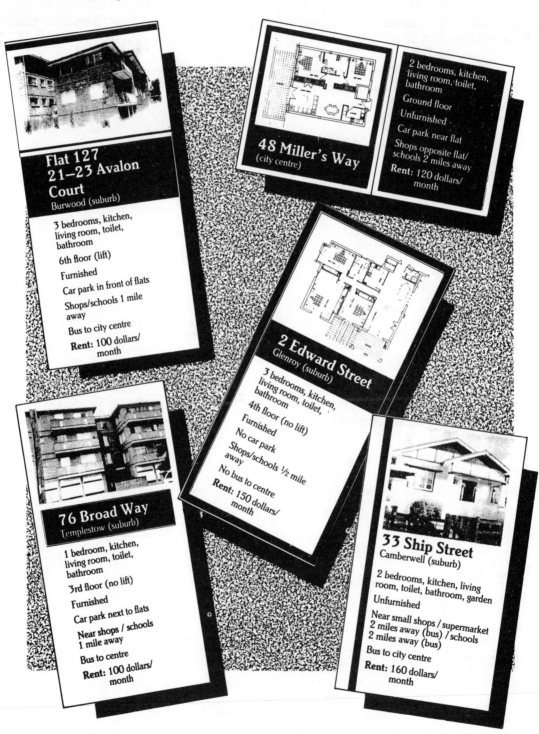

**Flat 127
21–23 Avalon
Court**
Burwood (suburb)

3 bedrooms, kitchen, living room, toilet, bathroom

6th floor (lift)

Furnished

Car park in front of flats

Shops/schools 1 mile away

Bus to city centre

Rent: 100 dollars/ month

---

48 Miller's Way
(city centre)

2 bedrooms, kitchen, living room, toilet, bathroom

Ground floor

Unfurnished

Car park near flat

Shops opposite flat/ schools 2 miles away

Rent: 120 dollars/ month

---

2 Edward Street
Glenroy (suburb)

3 bedrooms, kitchen, living room, toilet, bathroom

4th floor (no lift)

Furnished

No car park

Shops/schools ½ mile away

No bus to centre

Rent: 150 dollars/ month

---

76 Broad Way
Templestow (suburb)

1 bedroom, kitchen, living room, toilet, bathroom

3rd floor (no lift)

Furnished

Car park next to flats

Near shops / schools 1 mile away

Bus to centre

Rent: 100 dollars/ month

---

33 Ship Street
Camberwell (suburb)

2 bedrooms, kitchen, living room, toilet, bathroom, garden

Unfurnished

Near small shops / supermarket 2 miles away (bus) / schools 2 miles away (bus)

Bus to city centre

Rent: 160 dollars/ month

This is a quiz in a magazine. What exactly are the questions?

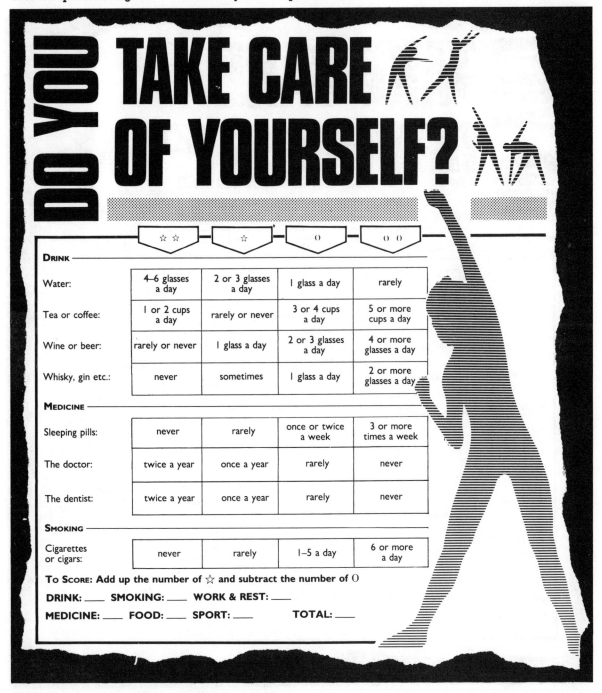

DO YOU TAKE CARE OF YOURSELF?

	☆ ☆	☆	O	O O
DRINK				
Water:	4–6 glasses a day	2 or 3 glasses a day	1 glass a day	rarely
Tea or coffee:	1 or 2 cups a day	rarely or never	3 or 4 cups a day	5 or more cups a day
Wine or beer:	rarely or never	1 glass a day	2 or 3 glasses a day	4 or more glasses a day
Whisky, gin etc.:	never	sometimes	1 glass a day	2 or more glasses a day
MEDICINE				
Sleeping pills:	never	rarely	once or twice a week	3 or more times a week
The doctor:	twice a year	once a year	rarely	never
The dentist:	twice a year	once a year	rarely	never
SMOKING				
Cigarettes or cigars:	never	rarely	1–5 a day	6 or more a day

To Score: Add up the number of ☆ and subtract the number of O

DRINK: ___ **SMOKING:** ___ **WORK & REST:** ___

MEDICINE: ___ **FOOD:** ___ **SPORT:** ___ **TOTAL:** ___

Find your score, then ask your partner the questions.

Your partner has the questions for 'Food', 'Work and Rest' and 'Sport'. Answer his questions to find your total score.

Is your score over 0? If not . . . !!!

This is a quiz in a magazine. What exactly are the questions?

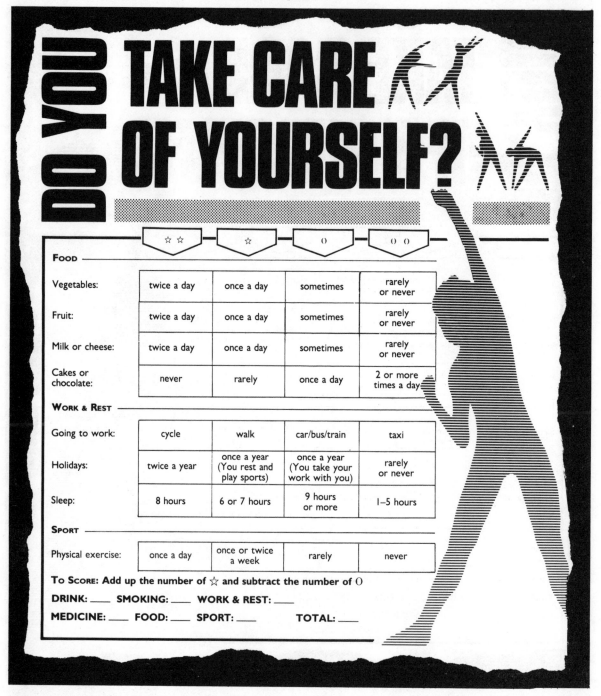

DO YOU TAKE CARE OF YOURSELF?

	☆☆	☆	O	O O
FOOD				
Vegetables:	twice a day	once a day	sometimes	rarely or never
Fruit:	twice a day	once a day	sometimes	rarely or never
Milk or cheese:	twice a day	once a day	sometimes	rarely or never
Cakes or chocolate:	never	rarely	once a day	2 or more times a day
WORK & REST				
Going to work:	cycle	walk	car/bus/train	taxi
Holidays:	twice a year	once a year (You rest and play sports)	once a year (You take your work with you)	rarely or never
Sleep:	8 hours	6 or 7 hours	9 hours or more	1–5 hours
SPORT				
Physical exercise:	once a day	once or twice a week	rarely	never

TO SCORE: Add up the number of ☆ and subtract the number of O

DRINK: ___ SMOKING: ___ WORK & REST: ___

MEDICINE: ___ FOOD: ___ SPORT: ___ TOTAL: ___

Find your score, then ask your partner the questions.

Your partner has the questions for 'Drink', 'Medicine' and 'Smoking'. Answer his questions to find your total score.

Is your score over 0? If not . . . !!!

What kind of person are you? Are you romantic? Do you prefer working alone or working with other people? What kind of books do you read?

There are four main kinds of people: Fire people, Air people, Earth people and Water people.

People with
FIRE SIGNS
They're very enthusiastic.

They're very interested in religion or politics.

They don't think carefully.

They're impatient.

People with
AIR SIGNS
They're interested in everything.

They often change their friends.

They have new ideas all the time.

They don't spend a lot of time with their families.

People with
EARTH SIGNS
They aren't impatient.

They like working alone.

They think carefully.

They don't often change their ideas.

People with
WATER SIGNS
They're very interested in dreams.

They're very romantic.

They're often unhappy.

They don't need order in their lives.

From *The Four Elements* by William Blake (1757–1827)

Which element (or elements) best describes your partner? Ask him the questions for Fire, Air, Earth and Water (e.g. 'Are you impatient?').

Are you sure his answers are correct? Ask him a second question, e.g. 'How often are you impatient?' 'Do you *ever* think carefully?' 'How much time do you spend with your family?'

Element signs (Fire, Earth, Air and Water) are very general, so there are twelve STAR SIGNS (three for Fire, three for Earth, etc.).

Find the three star signs for your partner's element sign (see page 51). Which of the three signs best describes him? Ask him the questions (e.g. 'Do you work slowly?').

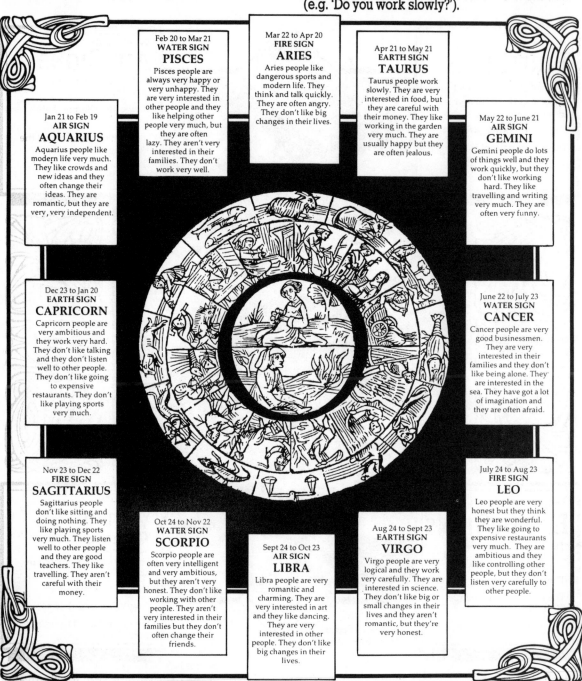

Feb 20 to Mar 21
WATER SIGN
PISCES
Pisces people are always very happy or very unhappy. They are very interested in other people and they like helping other people very much, but they are often lazy. They aren't very interested in their families. They don't work very well.

Mar 22 to Apr 20
FIRE SIGN
ARIES
Aries people like dangerous sports and modern life. They think and talk quickly. They are often angry. They don't like big changes in their lives.

Apr 21 to May 21
EARTH SIGN
TAURUS
Taurus people work slowly. They are very interested in food, but they are careful with their money. They like working in the garden very much. They are usually happy but they are often jealous.

Jan 21 to Feb 19
AIR SIGN
AQUARIUS
Aquarius people like modern life very much. They like crowds and new ideas and they often change their ideas. They are romantic, but they are very, very independent.

May 22 to June 21
AIR SIGN
GEMINI
Gemini people do lots of things well and they work quickly, but they don't like working hard. They like travelling and writing very much. They are often very funny.

Dec 23 to Jan 20
EARTH SIGN
CAPRICORN
Capricorn people are very ambitious and they work very hard. They don't like talking and they don't listen well to other people. They don't like going to expensive restaurants. They don't like playing sports very much.

June 22 to July 23
WATER SIGN
CANCER
Cancer people are very good businessmen. They are very interested in their families and they don't like being alone. They are interested in the sea. They have got a lot of imagination and they are often afraid.

Nov 23 to Dec 22
FIRE SIGN
SAGITTARIUS
Sagittarius people don't like sitting and doing nothing. They like playing sports very much. They listen well to other people and they are good teachers. They like travelling. They aren't careful with their money.

July 24 to Aug 23
FIRE SIGN
LEO
Leo people are very honest but they think they are wonderful. They like going to expensive restaurants very much. They are ambitious and they like controlling other people, but they don't listen very carefully to other people.

Oct 24 to Nov 22
WATER SIGN
SCORPIO
Scorpio people are often very intelligent and very ambitious, but they aren't very honest. They don't like working with other people. They aren't very interested in their families but they don't often change their friends.

Sept 24 to Oct 23
AIR SIGN
LIBRA
Libra people are very romantic and charming. They are very interested in art and they like dancing. They are very interested in other people. They don't like big changes in their lives.

Aug 24 to Sept 23
EARTH SIGN
VIRGO
Virgo people are very logical and they work very carefully. They are interested in science. They don't like big or small changes in their lives and they aren't romantic, but they're very honest.

When is your birthday? For example, if your birthday is between 24th October and 22nd November, you're a Scorpio. Did your partner find that sign for you?

Do you think your sign describes you well? Explain why and give examples.

4:00

You are a video controller in a department store. There is a video camera in every department, and you watch the customers. What is this woman doing?

Your partner is a detective. He is walking around the department store, looking for shop-lifters. Tell him about the woman.

The detective needs help. He can't see the woman — but which department is he in? Ask him, and then tell him what the shop-lifter is doing.

(These pictures of the shop-lifter are at different times, and they are not in order. Write the correct time in the box on the TV.)

TEACHER'S NOTE: You control the pace of the activity with a clock on the board. Don't let the students go on from one image to the next until you have changed the clock to the appropriate time. Students must be aware that these events are happening *now*.

You are a detective in a department store. You walk around the store and look for shop-lifters. There is a video camera in every department. Your partner is watching the customers on video.

Your partner can see a shop-lifter. What exactly is he (or she) doing? What does he (or she) look like? Ask your partner.

Now it's 4.10. You can't see the shop-lifter. Ask your partner. Can he see her?

TEACHER'S NOTE: You control the pace of the activity with a clock on the board. Don't let the students go on from one image to the next until you have changed the clock to the appropriate time. Students must be aware that these events are happening *now*.

You only know four of the people in this room. Your partner knows the other four people, but you can't ask 'Who's that?' and point. It's not very polite!

What can you ask? (What is he (or she) doing? wearing?)

Ask about their jobs and where they live too.

43 The High Road
Chiswick
London SW4
ENGLAND

David Lawrence
journalist
tel: 994 0385

18 rue Felix Faure
75005 Paris
FRANCE

PHILIPPE D'ARGENT
TAXI DRIVER
tel: 689 0516

2910 Lincoln Avenue
California 92801
U.S.A.

JO-ANNE MOODY
ENGINEER
tel: 258 5462

Turmstrasse 18
Bonn
WEST GERMANY

Nina Berg
doctor
tel: 960 4183

You only know four of the people in this room. Your partner knows the other four people, but you can't ask 'Who's that?' and point. It's not very polite!

What can you ask? (What is he (or she) doing? wearing?)

Ask about their jobs and where they live too.

21 Av. dé las Fuentes
Madrid
SPAIN

Laura Inclan

teacher

tel: 404 6614

18 via Magenta
Trastevere
Rome
ITALY

CARLO RAZO

Businessman

tel: 767 4112

John Carter
policeman

RR no. 8
Campbellville
Ontario LOP 1BU
CANADA

tel: 559 0109

98 Rawling Avenue
Camberwell
Melbourne
AUSTRALIA

Sheila Pickens

receptionist

tel: 981 0415

You are on holiday with your partner at the Mala Beach Hotel in Greece. You want to plan the next two days of your holiday.

This is a brochure about the hotel.

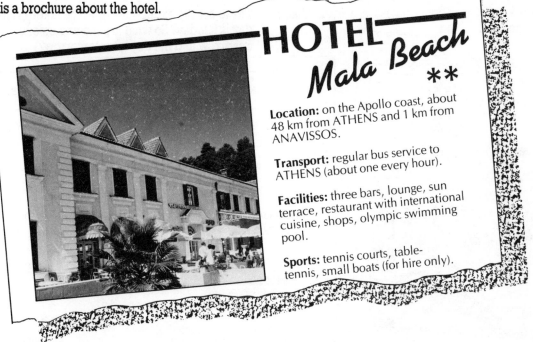

HOTEL Mala Beach **

Location: on the Apollo coast, about 48 km from ATHENS and 1 km from ANAVISSOS.

Transport: regular bus service to ATHENS (about one every hour).

Facilities: three bars, lounge, sun terrace, restaurant with international cuisine, shops, olympic swimming pool.

Sports: tennis courts, table-tennis, small boats (for hire only).

This is a notice in the hotel reception. (What day is it today? So what can you do at the hotel tomorrow and the day after tomorrow?)

```
This week in Hotel Mala Beach

* Dance music on the terrace
  every evening except
  Thursday.

* Discotheque on the beach on
  Wednesday and Sunday
  evenings.

* Thursday evening: Show of
  traditional Greek costumes and
  dancing (on the sun terrace).

* Greek lessons in the hotel
  lounge every day from 1:30 to
  2:30.
```

Your partner has information about Anavissos (a village near the hotel), and the excursions from the hotel. Ask him about them.

The village (Anavissos)
- night club?
- good restaurants?
- super market?
- souvenir shops?
- cinema?
Excursions
- tomorrow?
- the day after tomorrow?

What do you want to do tomorrow and the day after tomorrow? Talk with your partner and plan the two days *together*.

When you're ready, talk with other students in the class. Ask them about their plans. Tell them about your plans.

You are on holiday with your partner at the Mala Beach Hotel in Greece. You want to plan the next two days of your holiday.

This is a brochure about Anavissos, a small village near the hotel.

Anavissos

A small Greek fishing village with lots of romantic bars and restaurants. Try the *Loutraki* for its excellent fish and local wine. There is a market for fruit, vegetables and wine on Thursday and Saturday mornings.
A souvenir market is open every afternoon from 2 o'clock to 6 o'clock.

These are the excursions from the hotel. (What day is it today? So what are the excursions tomorrow and the day after tomorrow?)

EXCURSIONS	PRICES
Tuesday (all day) Athens: guided tour of the city, with visits to the Acropolis and the National Museum. Free afternoon for shopping.	800 DRS
Wednesday (evening) Barbecue: supper in a local farm with Greek dancing.	1300 DRS
Friday (evening) Athens by night: tour of the city by coach, and a dinner show in a small restaurant in the city centre.	1300 DRS
Sunday (all day) Boat trip to the islands: Hydra, Paros and Egine.	1680 DRS

Your partner has information about the Mala Beach Hotel. Ask him about it.

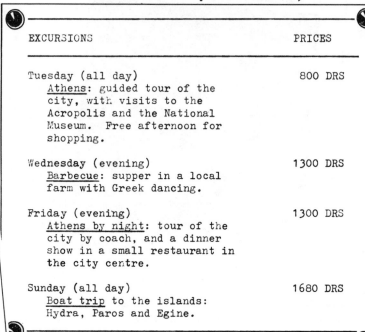

Hotel

Swimming Pool?
television room?
tennis courts?
discotheque?
anything else?
Anything interesting at the hotel tomorrow or the day after?

What do you want to do tomorrow and the day after tomorrow? Talk with your partner and plan the two days *together*.

When you're ready, talk with other students in the class. Ask them about their plans. Tell them about your plans.

You and your partner want to invite six people to a dinner party next weekend (5th or 6th May) or the weekend after that (12th or 13th May).

These are the six people you want to invite.

Karl and Cindy Owen
John Wilder
Debbie and Mark Harris
Melanie White

Are they free on one of the days?
If not, what are they doing?

Friday	5th MAY	Friday	12th MAY
Saturday	6th MAY	Saturday	13th MAY

These notes are on your desk.

Dear Sue,
    Could you babysit for us on Saturday 6th May? My parents are coming to visit us, and we'd like to take them out. Please let me know as soon as possible.
        Cindy

John Wilder
cordially invites
Sue Ryder
to a birthday party
on **Sat 6th May**
at **8.00 pm**
94 Beach Drive, Christchurch
Tel: 491058
R.S.V.P.

Dear Sue,
    We've got theatre tickets for "Angel City" on Friday 5th May. It starts at 7.00 pm and finishes quite early, at about 8.30. Would you like to come?
        Debbie & Mark

These notes are on a notice board at work.

We need three people to help us move to our new flat on 12th May from 6:30 to 8:00 pm (?). Can you help us? Please!
        Colin & Sarah
Paula Jones O.K.
Karl Owen O.K.
Bill Forsythe

CHRISTCHURCH TENNIS COURTS

Reservations: 12th May

TIME	COURT 1		COURT 2	
5-6 pm				
6-7 pm	Mark Huntington	+ David Walker	Maggie Smith	+ Ron Adams
7-8 pm	John Wilder	+ Melanie White		
8-9 pm	Peter Porter	+ Martin Hughes	Sally Morton	+ Lindsay Haynes
9-10 pm			Sally Hunt	+ James Lasden

Your partner has a few more notes. Ask him: When are your friends busy? free? If they're busy, what are they doing?

Find a day for the dinner party with your partner. Perhaps you can't invite everyone, or perhaps you can start the dinner party late.

You and your partner want to invite six people to a dinner party next weekend (5th or 6th May) or the weekend after that (12th or 13th May).

These are the six people you want to invite.

Karl and Cindy Owen
John Wilder
Debbie and Mark Harris
Melanie White

Friday 5th MAY	Friday 12th MAY
Saturday 6th MAY	Saturday 13th MAY

Are they free on one of the days?
If not, what are they doing?

These notes are on your desk.

Dear Andrew,
We're going to Helen's house for supper – Saturday after next (13th May) and Helen asked me to invite you as well. Can you come? Karl says please do, because he doesn't want to be the only man!
love,
Cindy

Dear Andrew,
I need your car to meet my brother at the station a week from Friday (12th May) His train arrives at 7.45 pm. Please?
Mark

These notes are on a notice board at work.

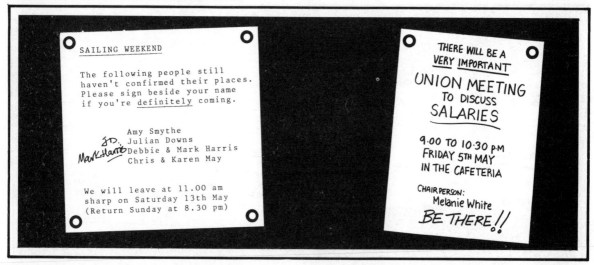

SAILING WEEKEND

The following people still haven't confirmed their places. Please sign beside your name if you're <u>definitely</u> coming.

Amy Smythe
JD. Julian Downs
Mark Harris Debbie & Mark Harris
Chris & Karen May

We will leave at 11.00 am sharp on Saturday 13th May (Return Sunday at 8.30 pm)

THERE WILL BE A VERY IMPORTANT
UNION MEETING
TO DISCUSS SALARIES

9.00 TO 10.30 P.M
FRIDAY 5TH MAY
IN THE CAFETERIA

CHAIRPERSON:
Melanie White
BE THERE!!

Your partner has a few more notes. Ask him:
When are your friends busy? free? If they're busy, what are they doing?

Find a day for the dinner party with your partner. Perhaps you can't invite everyone, or perhaps you can start the dinner party late.

You're at the cinema. The film this week is *The Bomb*. These are pictures from the film on a notice board outside the cinema.

THE BOMB: American colour, 1983, 1 hr 20 min, directed by Richard Briant, with Greta Jones, Richard Southern and Max de Viss.
A young airline pilot learns about a plot to kill a politician and tries to stop it.

Who's in the pictures? Where are they? What are they doing? Why are they doing that? If you don't know the answers, what do you think?

These are two parts of the film script. They aren't the parts for your pictures, but perhaps they can help you.

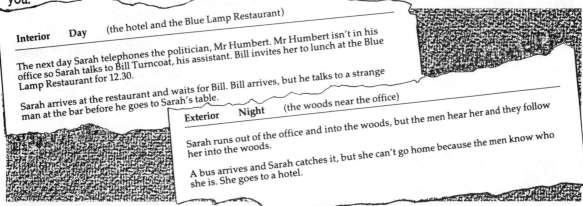

Interior   Day   (the hotel and the Blue Lamp Restaurant)

The next day Sarah telephones the politician, Mr Humbert. Mr Humbert isn't in his office so Sarah talks to Bill Turncoat, his assistant. Bill invites her to lunch at the Blue Lamp Restaurant for 12.30.

Sarah arrives at the restaurant and waits for Bill. Bill arrives, but he talks to a strange man at the bar before he goes to Sarah's table.

Exterior   Night   (the woods near the office)

Sarah runs out of the office and into the woods, but the men hear her and they follow her into the woods.

A bus arrives and Sarah catches it, but she can't go home because the men know who she is. She goes to a hotel.

1. Your partner has the parts of the film script for your pictures. Make a note of the questions you want to ask him.

You have the parts of the film script for your partner's pictures. What do you think is happening in his pictures?

2. When you're ready, talk with your partner. Show him your pictures and ask him about them. Also ask him what happens before and after them.

Answer his questions in your words. (Don't *read* the answers!)

Now you know about the first part of the film. Turn to page 64 and find out about the next part.

You're at the cinema. The film this week is *The Bomb*. These are pictures from the film on a notice board outside the cinema.

A M G CINEMA

THE BOMB

THE BOMB: American colour, 1983, 1 hr 20 min, directed by Richard Briant, with Greta Jones, Richard Southern and Max de Viss. A young airline pilot learns about a plot to kill a politician and tries to stop it.

Who's in the pictures? Where are they? What are they doing? Why are they doing that? If you don't know the answers, what do you think?

These are two parts of the film script. They aren't the parts for your pictures, but perhaps they can help you.

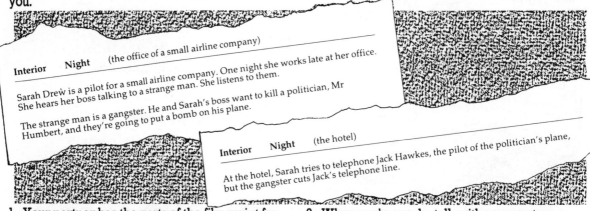

Interior   Night   (the office of a small airline company)

Sarah Drew is a pilot for a small airline company. One night she works late at her office. She hears her boss talking to a strange man. She listens to them.

The strange man is a gangster. He and Sarah's boss want to kill a politician, Mr Humbert, and they're going to put a bomb on his plane.

Interior   Night   (the hotel)

At the hotel, Sarah tries to telephone Jack Hawkes, the pilot of the politician's plane, but the gangster cuts Jack's telephone line.

1. Your partner has the parts of the film script for your pictures. Make a note of the questions you want to ask him.

You have the parts of the film script for your partner's pictures. What do you think is happening in his pictures?

2. When you're ready, talk with your partner. Show him your pictures and ask him about them. Also ask him what happens before and after them.

Answer his questions in your words. (Don't *read* the answers!)

Now you know about the first part of the film. Look at page 63 and find out about the next part.

AMG CINEMA

The BOMB

THE BOMB: American colour, 1983, 1 hr 20 min, directed by Richard Briant, with Greta Jones, Richard Southern and Max de Viss.
A young airline pilot learns about a plot to kill a politician and tries to stop it.

Work in the same way with these pictures and parts of the film script.

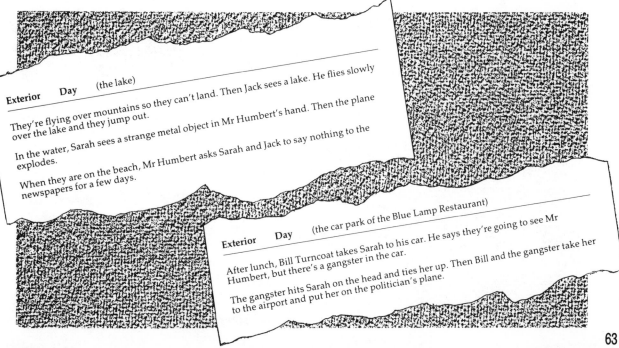

Exterior   Day   (the lake)

They're flying over mountains so they can't land. Then Jack sees a lake. He flies slowly over the lake and they jump out.

In the water, Sarah sees a strange metal object in Mr Humbert's hand. Then the plane explodes.

When they are on the beach, Mr Humbert asks Sarah and Jack to say nothing to the newspapers for a few days.

Exterior   Day   (the car park of the Blue Lamp Restaurant)

After lunch, Bill Turncoat takes Sarah to his car. He says they're going to see Mr Humbert, but there's a gangster in the car.

The gangster hits Sarah on the head and ties her up. Then Bill and the gangster take her to the airport and put her on the politician's plane.

AMG CINEMA

THE BOMB

THE BOMB: American colour, 1983, 1 hr 20 min, directed by Richard Briant, with Greta Jones, Richard Southern and Max de Viss.
    A young airline pilot learns about a plot to kill a politician, and tries to stop it.

Work in the same way with these pictures and parts of the film script.

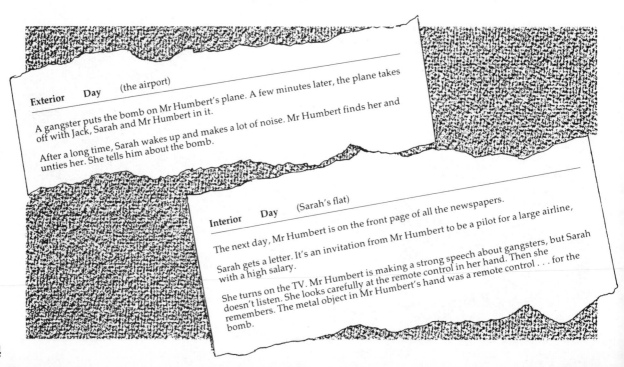

Exterior   Day   (the airport)

A gangster puts the bomb on Mr Humbert's plane. A few minutes later, the plane takes off with Jack, Sarah and Mr Humbert in it.

After a long time, Sarah wakes up and makes a lot of noise. Mr Humbert finds her and unties her. She tells him about the bomb.

Interior   Day   (Sarah's flat)

The next day, Mr Humbert is on the front page of all the newspapers.

Sarah gets a letter. It's an invitation from Mr Humbert to be a pilot for a large airline, with a high salary.

She turns on the TV. Mr Humbert is making a strong speech about gangsters, but Sarah doesn't listen. She looks carefully at the remote control in her hand. Then she remembers. The metal object in Mr Humbert's hand was a remote control . . . for the bomb.

The Sprach Schule König is a language school in Hamburg, Germany. Karen is a student there.

Roy: 22, beautiful but he's already got a girlfriend.

Hanseaten Weg 13
Grunwald
Hamburg

Dear Andrea,

Sorry this is typed, but I'm learning to use a German typewriter!

The school is lovely, and I'm really getting into it. There are eight students in my class, and some of them are very interesting, especially an American called Roy (but ... see photo!). The teachers are good too, and I really do feel my German is progressing.

The school building isn't much to write about. There are five classrooms - four are small and warm, and one is large and cold. (Guess which one I'm in. It's not fair!) All the furniture is new but it's very ugly and all the classrooms are very untidy. There's also a language lab but apparently it's always out of order so we never go there!

It's taken me ages to type this far, so I'll close here.

Lots of love,

Karen

P.S.
My teachers are Angelika and Klaus. Angelika is an excellent teacher, but she isn't very friendly. Klaus is very patient with me, but he's <u>boring</u>.

The Teachers
Wolfgang, Helga, Klaus, Peter, Angelika.

What's the school like? What about the teachers? the classrooms? the other students? the language lab? Anything else?

Colin was a student at the school in December 1981. Your partner has a letter from him. What was the school like then? What's different now?

The Sprach Schule König is a language school in Hamburg, Germany. Colin was a student there in December 1981.

The Teachers
Manfred Monika   Klaus Angelika
boring in class   impatient
but funny out   but
of class   interesting

Uschi, the receptionist
at the school. Beautiful!
young! not friendly!!(sigh!)

Jugendherberge
Zum Waldeck 14
Hamburg
10 Dec. 1981

Dear Michael,

Third day of classes and things are going quite well.

It's a very small school. There are only four small classrooms, but they're all warm and untidy - something I'd not expected from Germany with its reputation for fresh air and order.

There isn't a language lab or a tape-recorder or anything (the chairs and desks are very old), and the teachers don't really make up for it. But, to be fair, there are fourteen students in my class and the teachers really do try to make us all talk. (My teachers are Klaus and Monika - see photo.)

The real attraction of the school is Uschi, the receptionist. I asked her to show me how to use my polaroid properly. She did, with great patience and then looked unbelievingly at the botched effort I've enclosed. Oh well!

Will write again soon.

Yours
Colin

What was the school like in 1981? What about the teachers? the classrooms? the other students? the language lab? Anything else?

Karen is a student at the school now. Your partner has a letter from her. What's the school like now? What's new?

These were some of the students at Blue Hills High School in America. They left the school in 1976, and these were their plans.

The Class of '76

NANCY WRIGHT
Nancy is going to go to college in Ohio and become a teacher.

LINDA STODDARD
Linda is going to get married and have a baby. She wants to go to live in Boston, near her grandparents.

RON DALTON
Ron is going to go to New York and work in his uncle's shoe store.

KEM MONTGOMERY
Kem is going to work in the post office and sing in a rock group in his free time.

But did they do them? What do they do now?

Donald is writing a newsletter about the class of '76.

Scan this letter to him for some of the answers.

Dear Donald

Hi! Your idea of writing a newsletter about everyone in the class of '76 is great! I'd really love to know what everyone's doing now. How about a grand reunion next year?

My story first: I went to college in Ohio, but I left after two years because I didn't like it much. I'm a hairdresser now in Blue Hills. It's okay, but I'm too lazy to try to change jobs now!

John Philbrick got married to Sally, and they have two adorable children. He worked in the Heal Bank for three years. Then he got a job with the National Bank, and now he's assistant manager at the National Bank here in Blue Hills!

Steve Olsen went to Chicago. He was a journalist there for two years, but then he went to college and became a teacher. He teaches in Atlanta, Georgia now. I don't think he's married.

Virginia Brown wrote to me a couple of weeks ago. She went to medical school (in Texas, I think) and became a doctor <u>and</u> got married at medical school (her husband's a doctor too). They work in Brazil now in a little hospital in the mountains. Funny how people work out, isn't it!

That's all I know — I've lost touch with everyone else. Get that newsletter out!

Love, *Nancy.*

Your partner has another letter to Donald. What does he know about the students?

These were some of the students at Blue Hills High School in America. They left the school in 1976, and these were their plans.

The Class of '76

MARY FELDMANN
Mary is going to work in an office for a year. Then she's going to go to Australia and buy a farm.

VIRGINIA BROWN
Virginia is going to go to college in Oregon. She wants to become a doctor.

JOHN PHILBRICK
John is going to work in the Heal Bank here in Blue Hills and (yes!) he's going to marry Sally Price!!

STEVE OLSEN
Steve is going to stay in Blue Hills and become a journalist.

But did they do them? What do they do now?

Donald is writing a newsletter about the class of '76.

Scan this letter to him for some of the answers

Hi Donald,

I don't know how you managed to track me down but I'm sure glad you did. I got out the old yearbook when I got your letter and had a look at us young hopefuls. You've got to laugh at everything we wanted to do then!

I worked in an office but I didn't go to Australia. I got married instead. My husband's a bus driver. There wasn't much work in Blue Hills, so we moved to Pittsburgh, where we live with our four children.

Kem Montgomery went into the army after he left school. He was in the army for two years, but I'm not sure what he did after that. I know he's a pilot with Pan Am now. He got married to a Japanese woman last year, but I don't think they have any children yet.

Linda Stoddard got married, but she got divorced after two years (they didn't have any children). Then she went to college and studied computer science. She married again last year and she works for Maine Computers in Boston now.

Ron Dalton went to New York and worked in his uncle's shoe store. After three years he got married and bought a small clothes store. They visited me for a few days last summer, and they have the most adorable baby boy.

I don't know about anyone else. What's new with you? Come and see us next time you're in the area.

Yours

Mary Feldmann

Your partner has another letter to Donald. What does he know about the students?

Last week your boss sent you to a seminar at the Java Hotel in Singapore, but you didn't go. You went out with a friend instead, and had a very good time!

Thursday 12

Island Restaurant
49–52 Sea Walk
Singapore

2 crab salads	3	00
1 baked fish	6	00
1 roast chicken	5	50
1 special ice-cream	2	50
1 fruit salad	2	00
2 coffees	8	
1 bottle of wine	5	0
	24	50

Friday 13

Home at 5 in the morning, after a great evening! 'West Side Story.' (It was good, but I prefer the film). Then an excellent supper (wonderful crab salad!) Then 3 hours of dancing!! It's a good thing tomorrow's Saturday!

THE
CHINA GATE THEATRE
PRESENTS
WEST SIDE STORY
13 September
6:45pm
$15.00
D19

CHUN'S Discotheque

93 RAFFLES AVENUE
SINGAPORE

OPEN 10.00pm–5.00am

But yesterday your boss sent you this note.

Can you write a report about the seminar last week please? Jack

What can you do? ... Your partner was at the seminar.

(On page 10 there is an article about a *different* seminar. Use it to give you ideas for questions.)

Last week you went to a seminar at the Java Hotel in Singapore. This was the programme, with your notes.

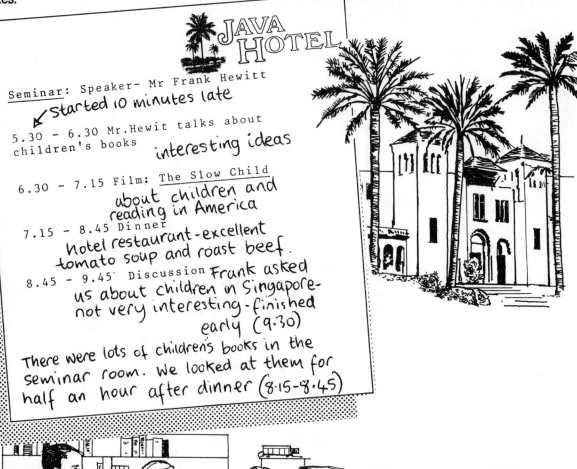

Seminar: Speaker- Mr Frank Hewitt

↙ Started 10 minutes late

5.30 – 6.30 Mr.Hewit talks about children's books   interesting ideas

6.30 – 7.15 Film: The Slow Child
about children and reading in America

7.15 – 8.45 Dinner
hotel restaurant-excellent tomato soup and roast beef.

8.45 – 9.45 Discussion Frank asked us about children in Singapore- not very interesting-finished early (9.30)

There were lots of children's books in the seminar room. We looked at them for half an hour after dinner (8.15-8.45)

You were surprised because your partner wasn't at the seminar. Why not? What did he do instead? Ask him for details.

QUICK CAR HIRE

You are the manager of Quick Car Hire. These people work in your office.

HELEN STONE

ALAN SHIPWAY

ANNE JAMES

SUSAN WILDER

MARK JONES

CHARLES ROLLINS

Yesterday you got a letter from a customer. He was very angry . . .

Dear Sir,

I rarely complain about service, but I have never been treated with the rudeness and disrespect I met this morning at your Holly Road branch.

Nobody helped me. Two people were eating sandwiches and drinking coffee. One person was talking to a friend on the phone – I'm sure it was a friend because he was laughing and talking about a party. Another person was reading a newspaper, and when I asked her if she could help me, she directed me vaguely towards an empty desk! One woman was talking to a young man, and the young man was sitting on her desk. Only one person was working, and she was counting money at the back of the room! If this goes on, I'm sure she will have less and less to count.

I'm afraid that neither I nor my friends will go to Quick Car Hire again, so I shall never know if the service improves. For other tourists like myself, I can only hope it does.

Yours faithfully,

Reginald Dewey

Reginald Dewey

. . .but what can you do? Who was eating sandwiches? Who was reading a newspaper? Was it Charles Rollins or Helen Stone or . . .? The customer didn't describe the person (e.g. 'A man with fair, curly hair was reading a newspaper') so you don't know.

Another customer (your partner) is going to telephone you. This time, ask for descriptions and make notes.

Yesterday you wanted to rent a car. You went to Quick Car Hire and saw this.

They didn't help you. You waited for fifteen minutes, and then you left. You were very angry!

This morning you started to write a letter to the manager . . .

Dear Sir,

I went to Quick Car Hire in Holly Road yesterday because I wanted to rent a car. It was a **very** bad idea.

When I arrived at 11.30, **nobody** was working and **nobody** helped me.
One man was talking and took no notice of me.
Another man ... up who...

. . .but then you decided to telephone him. Your partner is the manager.

These are notes for an article about Marta Lenska.

```
MARTA LENSKA

BORN:        Poland    when?

MARRIED:     Greff Lenska (Engineer)   when?

EDUCATION:   School (1926 - 1935)
             University (1955 - 1962)  studied what?

LIVED:       Poland (1921 - 1945)
             Italy (1945 -      )  how long?
             Libya (      -      )  ?
             America (1971 - 1980)

VISITED:     1974 -     ← where?
             1975 - Africa

JOBS:        1962 - 1971 Doctor
             1971 - 1980    ← job?

BOOKS:       Italian Cooking (    )  ?
             Waiting for Rain (1964) ← about what?
             Their World (1979)
                (about children and food)

DIED:        1980    where?
```

A lot of the information is missing. Your partner has an article about Marta Lenska. Can he answer your questions?

What happened in the world or in your country during Marta Lenska's life?

Your partner wants to know about Charles Morton. This is an article about him.

THIS MONTH IN NEW YORK

There is an excellent exhibition of photographs by Charles Morton at the Central Museum. Don't miss it.

Charles Morton was born in India in 1906. In 1922 he left India and went to London. He was a journalist with the *Daily Mail* in London for six years.

In 1930 he left the *Daily Mail* and married Janet Owen. Charles, Janet and three friends started a news agency, 'World News', in 1931. The agency sold photographs and articles to newspapers.

From 1932 to '38 Charles lived and worked in the Middle East and India, sending his photographs and articles to 'World News' in England.

He wrote two books, *Iran*, in 1936, and *Changes*, a book about India, in 1938.

He visited Algeria for three months in 1938, and then he went to Turkey and lived there for four years. He died in Beirut in 1942.

These are notes for an article about Charles Morton.

```
CHARLES MORTON

born:          1906        IN INDIA ?

nationality:   English

married:       1930        WHO ?

education:     school 1912 - 1922 ( in India )

lived:         India (1906 - 1922)    ?
               England (    -    )    ?
               Middle East (1932 - 1938)
               Turkey (1938 -    )   HOW LONG ?

visited:       1937 India
               1938       WHERE ?

jobs:          journalist:  Daily Mail (1924 -    )  ?
                            World News (1931 - 1938 )
                                ← A NEWSPAPER ?

books:         Iran (1936)
               Changes (    ) ? ABOUT WHAT ?

died:          Beirut (    ) ?
```

A lot of the information is missing. Your partner has an article about Charles Morton. Can he answer your questions?

What happened in the world or in your country during Charles Morton's life?

Your partner wants to know about Marta Lenska. This article is in the front of her book, *Their World*.

THEIR WORLD

About the author, *Marta Lenska*:

MARTA Lenska was born in Poland in 1921. She left school in 1935 and married Greff Lenska, an engineer. She and her husband went to Italy in 1945 and lived near Milan. In 1951 she wrote *Italian Cooking*.

In 1952 they visited Libya for six months. Marta often went to the villages and ate with the people there. When they returned to Italy, Marta went to university and studied medicine.

She left Italy in 1962 and went to live in Libya. She was a doctor there for nine years. In 1964 she wrote *Waiting for Rain*, a book about food problems in Africa.

In 1971 she went to America and worked for the United Nations. She visited countries in South America (1974) and Africa (1975) and studied food problems there. She wrote *Their World* in 1979. She died in New York in 1980.

Mr Knight wrote to Carter's Mail Order and asked for their catalogue. They sent the catalogue to him on 10th February.

After that, on 23rd February, Mr Knight sent this letter to Carter's Mail Order.

Only these parts of the letter are correct.

```
                                        25 Lexden Road
                                        Sevenoaks
                                        Kent

                                        23rd February, 1985

The Sales Manager
Carter's Mail Order
435-8 The Precinct
Colchester
Essex CO3 3QP

Dear Sir,

I got your letter of 10th February with your 1985 catalogue
in it.  Thank you very much.  Send one men's jacket,
catalogue no. BS412, at once.  A cheque for £8.99 is in
this envelope.

I look forward to hearing from you soon.

Yours faithfully,

    A Knight

Albert Knight  (Mr)
```

```
                        The Box Office
                        The Shaw Theatre
                        90 Charing Cross Road
  25 Lexden Road        London WC2
  Sevenoaks
  Kent



Dear Mr,
     Your letter of 21st January with two tickets for Romeo and
Juliet in it arrived in the post last week.  Thank you very much.
Send two tickets at £4.60 for Coriolanus on April 2nd at once.
There is a cheque for £9.20 in this envelope.

     Please answer soon.

     Lots of love,

    A Knight



  6th February 1985
```

Correct the same parts of this letter from Mr Knight to the Shaw Theatre.

What do you think is the correct form for the message in these letters?

Ask your partner about it.

Mrs Evelyn Drew wrote to Carter's Mail Order and asked for their catalogue. They sent the catalogue to her on 25th May.

After that, on 1st June, Mrs Drew sent this letter to Carter's Mail Order.

Only this part of the letter is correct.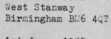

```
                                    The Sales Manager
                                    Carters Mail Order
        42 Alders Court             435-8 The Precinct
        West Stanway                Colchester
        Birmingham BM6 4QT          Essex CO3 3QP

        1st June, 1985

        Dear Mr,

        Thank you for your letter of 25th May enclosing
        your 1985 catalogue.

        Please send two skirts, catalogue nos. FS412 and
        FS816, as soon as possible.

        A cheque for £9.98 is enclosed.

        Write back soon.

        Love,

           E.Drew .
```

```
        42 Alders Court
        West Stanway
        Birmingham BM6 4QT

        The Box Office
        Shaw Theatre
        90 Charing Cross Rd.
        LONDON WC2

        Mr,

        I got your letter of 23rd April with 4 tickets for Hamlet in it.
        Send two tickets at £5.40 for A Midsummer Night's Dream on June
        29th at once.  There is a cheque for £10.80 in this envelope.

        Please answer soon.

        Goodbye,

           E.Drew .

        2nd May, 1985
```

Correct the same part of this letter from Mrs Drew to the Shaw Theatre.

What do you think is the correct form for the rest of these letters?

Ask your partner about it.

You're going on a business trip next Thursday. Before you leave, you have three days (Monday, Tuesday and Wednesday) to do the things on this list.

Which things do you have to do? Which things would you like to do?

Prepare a diary for the three days. You can only do these things at lunch time (12.30 to 14.00) and after work (after 18.00).

Now make an appointment with your partner for one of the days. You need at least an hour together.

Don't accept 'No' easily. If your partner says he's busy, check: What's he doing? Does he have to do it then? Can he do it another day?

To do before Thursday:
- *Dentist (Tues. 12.30)*
- *Monday: be at home by 7.30p.m. (parents coming to dinner)*
- *Collect the car from Old's Garage. (after work on Monday if possible, by wed. evening at the latest)*
- *Meeting with the Sales Manager. (Wed. 5.30 to 7.30)*
- *shopping: new suitcase, rolls of film.*

TRAVEL REGULATIONS IN THE UNITED KINGDOM

VISAS
Visas are not required of visitors to the U.K. from an E.E.C. country.

INTERNATIONAL DRIVING LICENCE
It is not compulsory to have an international driving licence. Foreign driving licences are valid for one year.

MOTORWAYS
You are not required to pay to go on motorways. The maximum speed limit is 70 m.p.h.

SAFETY BELTS
The wearing of safety belts while travelling in the front seat of a car is compulsory at all times.

MEDICAL CARE
The D.H.S.S. (Social Security) pays for medical care for residents and visitors.

The business trip is to Paris.

These are the travel regulations for the United Kingdom. What are they exactly? ('It is compulsory' and 'you are required' = 'you have to...')

Are they the same in France? Ask your partner.

You're going on a business trip next Thursday. Before you leave, you have three days (Monday, Tuesday and Wednesday) to do the things on this list.

Which things do you have to do? Which things would you like to do?

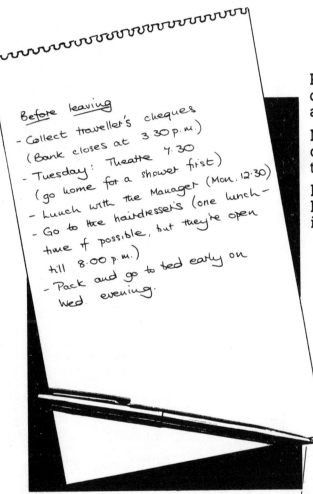

Before leaving
- Collect traveller's cheques
  (Bank closes at 3.30 p.m.)
- Tuesday: Theatre 7.30
  (go home for a shower first)
- Lunch with the Manager (Mon. 12.30)
- Go to the hairdresser's (one lunch-
  time if possible, but they're open
  till 8.00 p.m.)
- Pack and go to bed early on
  Wed. evening.

Prepare a diary for the three days. You can only do these things at lunchtime (12.30 to 14.00) and after work (after 18.00).

Now make an appointment with your partner for one of the days. You need at least an hour together.

Don't accept 'No' easily. If your partner says he's busy, check: What's he doing? Does he have to do it then? Can he do it another day?

TRAVEL REGULATIONS IN FRANCE

VISAS
Visas are not required of visitors to France from an E.E.C. country.

INTERNATIONAL DRIVING LICENCE
It is not compulsory to have an international driving licence. Foreign driving licences are valid for one year.

MOTORWAYS
You are required to pay to go on all motorways. The amount you pay depends on the distance you have to travel. The maximum speed limit is 130 k.p.h.

SAFETY BELTS
The wearing of safety belts while travelling in the front seat of a car is compulsory at all times.

MEDICAL CARE
The Social Security pays 70% of medical costs for *residents only*. Visitors should take out an insurance.

The business trip is to London.

These are the travel regulations for France. What are they exactly? ('It is compulsory' and 'you are required' = 'you have to ...')

Are they the same in the United Kingdom? Ask your partner.

Diana is an au pair with the Moretti family in Rome (Italy). She wants to leave the job, and she wrote this letter to a friend.

Why does she want to leave? (Make notes: What things does she have to do? Does she like doing them? What else does she like or dislike?)

C/O Moretti
33 via Cassia
Trastevere
Roma

12 October

Dear Alice,

I'm thinking of leaving my job with the Morettis. A number of things are starting to get on my nerves and I don't think they'll improve.

Mrs Moretti is quite nice, but I have to speak English all the time with her, and I want to practise my Italian. Mr Moretti speaks Italian with me, but I don't like him at all. He's a bit too friendly sometimes.

Both parents leave for work at 8.00, so I have to get up very early (7.30!!) and take Marco to school. Then I have to do the housework and cook dinner before Mr and Mrs Moretti arrive home. I quite like cooking but not every day! And I hate housework.

The job isn't all bad. I have to play with Marco after school, but I like that a lot and he has a lovely accent when he tries to speak English!

As for my room, it's cold and ugly, but it's on the top floor (the Moretti's flat is on the third floor) and I like being independent.

Still, if I stay I won't see any of Rome or Italian life. Catherine has offered me a place on her floor while I'm looking round, and I think I'll accept.

All love,

Diana

My Room - Cold ugly but _independent_

Marco - 7 years old bad - but funny !!

Diana saw this advertisement a few days ago.

Another girl, Marleen, was an au pair for Mrs Citto last year. Your partner has a letter from her.

Ask your partner about the job, for example: Did Marleen have to speak English? What was the family like? etc.
Then decide together if Diana should take the new job.

Marleen is now an English teacher in Rome. Ask your partner about her job.

Mrs Citto is looking for an English au pair

tel. 486 04 11

Last year, Marleen was an au pair with the Citto family in Rome (Italy).
She wrote this letter about the job to a friend.
(Make notes: What did she have to do? What's the family like?)

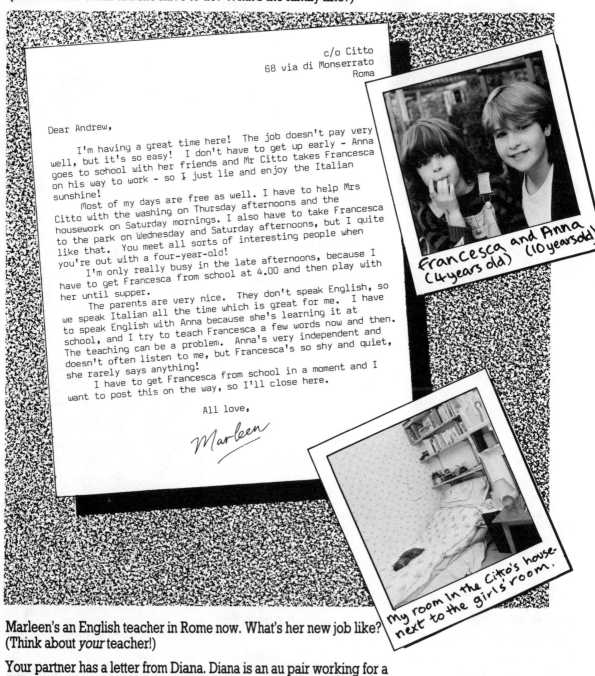

c/o Citto
68 via di Monserrato
Roma

Dear Andrew,

I'm having a great time here! The job doesn't pay very well, but it's so easy! I don't have to get up early - Anna goes to school with her friends and Mr Citto takes Francesca on his way to work - so I just lie and enjoy the Italian sunshine!

Most of my days are free as well. I have to help Mrs Citto with the washing on Thursday afternoons and the housework on Saturday mornings. I also have to take Francesca to the park on Wednesday and Saturday afternoons, but I quite like that. You meet all sorts of interesting people when you're out with a four-year-old!

I'm only really busy in the late afternoons, because I have to get Francesca from school at 4.00 and then play with her until supper.

The parents are very nice. They don't speak English, so we speak Italian all the time which is great for me. I have to speak English with Anna because she's learning it at school, and I try to teach Francesca a few words now and then. The teaching can be a problem. Anna's very independent and doesn't often listen to me, but Francesca's so shy and quiet, she rarely says anything!

I have to get Francesca from school in a moment and I want to post this on the way, so I'll close here.

All love,

Marleen

*francesca and Anna
(4 years old) (10 years old)*

*my room in the Citto's house-
next to the girls' room.*

Marleen's an English teacher in Rome now. What's her new job like?
(Think about *your* teacher!)

Your partner has a letter from Diana. Diana is an au pair working for a different family, the Morettis, but she doesn't like her job.

Mrs Citto is looking for a new au pair. Should Diana work for her?
(Discuss with your partner: Why is Diana unhappy in her present job?
Would she prefer working for the Citto family?)

You're a journalist. You have to interview Reg Fisher, the actor. (He's going to be in a play in Evesham Theatre soon.) You asked your colleagues about Reg Fisher. They told you:

—JOURNALIST'S—
PRESS PASS

Is the information correct? Your partner has a recent article about Reg Fisher, so check your information with him and ask him the other questions on the list.

Reg Fisher
- Scottish
- was in the film The Sound of Music
- is in "Andy and Co" (What is it?!) on TV.
- sings very badly (!)
- went to school in Evesham.
- has a large house near Cardiff.

spare time? prefers theatre or television? relaxed? talks a lot?

Your partner has to interview Carol Roberts and he's going to ask you about her. Use this article to answer his questions. (Mrs Roberts likes interviews and is usually very relaxed and friendly.)

CAROL ROBERTS MAYOR?

Will Mrs Carol Roberts be the first woman mayor of Evesham? A lot of people think so. Our reporter went to see her at her home in Didbourne, a small village northeast of Evesham.

You're a teacher, aren't you, Mrs Roberts?
ROBERTS: Not exactly, I'm really a solicitor. I studied law at Cambridge, and I worked in a solicitor's office for three years, but I didn't like the job.
So you started teaching at Evesham High School?
ROBERTS: Yes, that's right. Teaching was more interesting and I like the High School. I went there for two years when I was a girl, you know. My daughter's at the school now.
Yes, you've got three children, haven't you?
ROBERTS: Yes, I have, but I don't see them very often. Sometimes I play tennis or go horse-riding with them, but I haven't got much free time. I'm too busy!
With the Links Organization, for example. Can you tell me about that?

ROBERTS: The Links Organization helps people to start new companies. I started the organization in 1979 with my husband, a businessman, because we felt that our joint experience could help people with good ideas to

You're a journalist. You have to interview Carol Roberts, the new mayor at Evesham (near Bristol). You asked your colleagues about Carol Roberts. They told you:

JOURNALIST'S
PRESS PASS

Is the information correct? Your partner has a recent article about Carol Roberts, so check your information with him and ask him the other questions on the list.

Your partner has to interview Mr Fisher and he's going to ask you about him. Use this article to answer his questions. (Reg Fisher isn't very relaxed at interviews, but he talks a lot.)

Carol Roberts
- *teacher*
- *lives in a small village outside Evesham*
- *started an organisation (name?) - (what does it do?)*
- *has 2 children*
- *was deputy mayor 3 years ago.*
- *went to Evesham High School*

husband's job?
spare time?
friendly?
likes interviews?

REG & CO.

REG FISHER plays the father of a large family in 'Andy & Co.', the new television comedy series. Our reporter went to see him at his London home.

Mr. Fisher . . .
FISHER: Call me Reg.
Fine. You're Scottish aren't you, Reg?
FISHER: Yes, that's right. My parents come from Glasgow, and I lived there until I left school at 16. I'd like to live there again one day, and work in a theatre there.
Do you prefer the theatre to films or television?
FISHER: Oh yes. I was in one film, *Up to Heaven*, a few years ago, but I didn't enjoy it. Television pays better and it's fun sometimes, but I'm happiest in the theatre.

What do you do when you are not acting? You play a lot of sports, don't you?
FISHER: No, not really. I go jogging every morning and sometimes I play football with friends, but I prefer reading or travelling in my spare time. I also enjoy staying at my sister's house near Cardiff. There are woods and hills behind the house which are perfect for long walks with my children.

This advertisement was in a London newspaper recently.

ASSISTANT PHOTOGRAPHER

to join an expedition to

BRAZIL

Applicants must be over 25 and have some experience of

ANIMAL PHOTOGRAPHY

Applications to: Sue Reynolds
Shepherd Films
43 Ringway Cres
London E3

Sue Reynolds also had these notes from the leader of the expedition.

> I want someone with experience of living in a hot country and working with animals. If possible, he (or she) should also have some experience of Brazil, expeditions, driving a truck and using a 2-way radio.
>
> He (or she) should also speak Portuguese, climb well and swim well.
>
> GOOD LUCK!!!!!!

Jerome Cawley has had an interview for the job. These are his Curriculum Vitae, a photograph, and the interviewer's notes.

Is he right for the job? (Has he ever lived in a hot country? If he has, where? How long? etc.

CURRICULUM VITAE

Name	Jerome Cawley
Nationality	British (English)
Address	49 Downs Road, Bristol 7
Marital Status	Single
Date of birth	16th February, 1956

Higher Education

1974 Advanced Levels in Biology and Mathematics at Bristol Grammar School.

1979-80 Photography course at the Royal School of Arts, London.

Professional Experience

1974-76 Assistant at Bristol Zoo.

1976-79 Journalist with the <u>Bristol Evening Post</u>.

1980 Work for a BBC television documentary taking underwater pictures of fish in the Mediterranean Sea.

At the moment I am an independent photographer. I occasionally work for the magazines <u>Time Out</u> and <u>The Face</u>.

Interests

In 1977 I drove across the Sahara desert with friends. (2 months)

Sports include swimming and table tennis.

Jerome Cowley
- quiet, thinks quickly
- has never visited a country outside Europe, except for the Sahara trip.
- drove a truck on the Sahara trip.
- no experience of 2-way radios.

Your partner has got information about another applicant, Helen Maynard. Decide together which applicant is best. (Remember: certain experience or abilities are more important for this job than others.)

This advertisement was in a London newspaper recently.

ASSISTANT PHOTOGRAPHER

to join an expedition to

BRAZIL

Applicants must be over 25 and have some experience of

ANIMAL PHOTOGRAPHY

Applications to: Sue Reynolds
Shepherd Films
43 Ringway Cres
London E3

Sue Reynolds also had these notes from the leader of the expedition.

I want someone with experience of living in a hot country and working with animals. If possible, he (or she) should also have some experience of Brazil, expeditions, driving a truck and using a 2-way radio.

He (or she) should also speak Portuguese, climb well and swim well.

GOOD LUCK!!!!!!

Helen Maynard has had an interview for the job. These are her Curriculum Vitae, a photograph, and the interviewer's notes.

Is she right for the job? (Has she ever lived in a hot country? If she has, where? How long? etc.)

Helen Maynard
- charming and enthusiastic
- her photographs of animals in Ghana are excellent.
- the Ghana job included driving a truck and using a 2-way radio.

CURRICULUM VITAE

NAME: Helen Maynard   **NATIONALIITY:** British (Scottish)

ADDRESS: 36 Ardington Lane London W4   **MARITAL STATUS:** Single

DATE OF BIRTH: 12.4.57

HIGHER EDUCATION

1975	Advanced Levels in French, Spanish and Geography Edinburgh High School
1979	BA Degree in Spanish and Portuguese Manchester University
1981-82	Photography Course Royal School of Arts, London

PROFESSIONAL EXPERIENCE

1979-81	Work in Ghana, Africa , helping look after animals on a game reserve.
1982-83	Independent photographer in London.
Present	Assistant to David Bowles, fashion photographer.

INTERESTS

Sports including rock climbing.

Your partner has got information about another applicant, Jerome Cawley. Decide together which applicant is best. (Remember: certain experience or abilities are more important for this job than others.)

8.10 — Top Of T
8.50 — Points
Barry
throug
letters
9.00 — News; V
9.25 — M i a m
"Nobody
ever". Cr
Tubbs ar.
to homic
three ps
teenag
throug
10.15 — The
Film G
11.45 — Weath

What
six
often
can-
does
usic
ia a
The
all in
ramme
series
how
search
dlands

This evening: The continuing drama of *Los Angeles* (episode 56)

Los Angeles is a television serial about the Holt family.

The parents (picture centre) live on a ranch outside Los Angeles.

They have four children: (from left to right at top) Billy and his wife Sue; Becky and her husband Tom; Mark; (bottom left) Linda.

This is the situation so far (the end of the last episode).

Billy and Sue

Mark

Linda

Becky and Tom

Billy, Becky and Mrs Holt

Mr Holt

The next episode is on TV at the moment, but you've missed half of it. Your partner has watched the episode from the beginning, so ask him what has happened to Becky, Linda, etc.

This evening: The continuing drama of Los Angeles (episode 56)

8.50 — Poi...
Barry
throug'
letters
9.00 — News; V
9.25 — Mian
"Nobody
ever". Cr
Tubbs ar.
to homic
three ps/
teenag
throug'
10.15 — The
Fil...
11

Los Angeles is a television serial about the Holt family.

The parents (picture centre) live on a ranch outside Los Angeles.

They have four children: (from left to right at top) Billy and his wife Sue; Becky and her husband Tom; Mark; (bottom left) Linda.

An episode of **Los Angeles** is on TV at the moment. You have watched it from the beginning, and you have seen this.

Mark

Mark

Billy

Billy and Sue

Becky

Becky

Linda and Mrs Holt

Mr Holt

Mr Holt

Your partner has missed half the episode and he's going to ask you what has happened.

1. This graph shows income tax in Maro (an island in the Pacific Ocean).

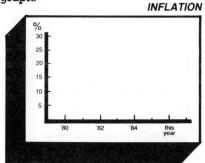

What are the missing words?

> **Income Tax** was _____ 27% at the beginning of 1979. It went down _____ 25% in 1980, and then it went up _____ 30% in 1981. It went down _____ 21% in 1982 and it stayed _____ 21% for two years. Since then it has gone up _____ 25%.

Ask your partner about inflation in Maro and draw the graph.

INFLATION

UNEMPLOYMENT

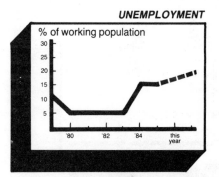

2. There are two political parties in Maro, the Green party and the White party. The Green party was in government for three years, from the end of 1978 to the end of 1981. The White party has been in government since then.

– The Green government increased income tax from 27% to 30%. What did it do about unemployment and inflation?

– The White government has reduced income tax from 30% to 25%. What has it done about unemployment and inflation?

3. The Green government also did these things.

The Green Government

Feb. 1979:	Cut spending on the army.
June 1979:	Nationalized the clothing industry.
Dec. 1979:	Bought three war ships from Great Britain.
July 1979–Aug. 1981:	Built 42 hospitals.
Apr. 1980:	Increased subsidies to schools.
Sept. 1981:	Increased subsidies to the fishing industry.

Ask your partner about the White government. What has it done about public spending? defence spending? industry?

1. This graph shows income tax in Maro (an island in the Pacific Ocean).

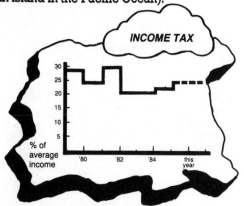

% of average income

What are the missing words?

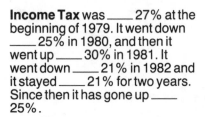

Income Tax was ____ 27% at the beginning of 1979. It went down ____ 25% in 1980, and then it went up ____ 30% in 1981. It went down ____ 21% in 1982 and it stayed ____ 21% for two years. Since then it has gone up ____ 25%.

Ask your partner about unemployment in Maro and draw the graph.

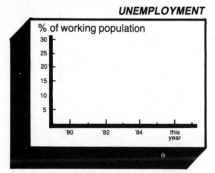

UNEMPLOYMENT

% of working population

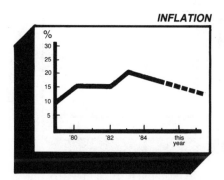

INFLATION

2. There are two political parties in Maro, the Green party and the White party. The Green party was in government for three years, from the end of 1978 to the end of 1981. The White party has been in government since then.

3. The White government has also done these things.

– The Green govenment increased income tax from 27% to 30%. What did it do about unemployment and inflation?

– The White government has reduced income tax from 30% to 25%. What has it done about unemployment and inflation?

THE WHITE GOVERNMENT

March.	1982:	Cut subsidies to the fishing industry.
Nov.	1982:	Increased spending on the army.
Jan.	1983:	Cut subsidies to schools.
Apr.	1984:	Bought ten fighter planes from America.
May	1984:	Nationalized the steel industry.
Sept.	1982–Oct. 1985:	Built an underground (railway) in the capital city.

Ask your partner about the Green government. What did it do about public spending? defence spending? industry?

Lentz is an island in the Indian Ocean. There are two political parties in Lentz: the Sky party and the Wave party.

The Sky party was in government from 1978 to 1982. What happened to income tax, inflation, unemployment, public spending, defence spending and industry under the Sky government? This article was in the *Lentz Times* in 1982, just before the elections.

INCOME TAX

% of average income

'76 '78 '80

Sky Government

INFLATION

%

'76 '78 '80

Sky Government

UNEMPLOYMENT

% of working population

'76 '78 '80

Sky Government

BM CAPRI
ATHROOM
SUITE
W ONLY
£299

industrial and military fields. On an international level this has met with some success (see article by Tao Rudi, p. 48) but domestically the results have been — to put it kindly — mixed.

Public Spending
The sink-or-swim policy adopted by the government has not been applied with quite as much rigour as initially suggested. The Sky government has cut subsidies to the glass and steel industries, but less than anticipated. The compromise has avoided closure of these industries but left them without sufficient funds to reinvest and streamline effectively. Their future is far from certain.

On a social level, the Sky government has cut subsidies to schools, especially in rural areas. With no coherent philosophy behind the cuts, technical subjects have disappeared in favour of traditional (and less costly) academic subjects. The long-term results of this situation for industrial development in Lentz

The government has also built a lot of new roads in Lentz, most of them capable of taking a medium flow of industrial traffic. The result has been a significant improvement in communications but has favoured imports of foreign vehicles at the cost of our indigenous — and labour intensive — railway industry.

Defence Spending
The airforce and the navy have done well out of the present government. The Sky government has bought 42 fighter planes from the French Government over the past four years, and it bought five war ships from the Americans in 1979. The success of the army in suppressing the popular uprising in the Char Province last year has theless left

The Wave party won the elections in 1982, and it is still in government. What has it done about income tax? Has inflation gone up? etc.

Ask your partner and compare the two governments.

There will be an election next month. Discuss with your partner: What are the problems in Lentz at the moment? What should the new government do about public spending, etc.? Which party should be elected?

Lentz is an island in the Indian Ocean. There are two political parties in Lentz: the Sky party and the Wave party.

The Wave party has been in government since 1982. What has happened to income tax, inflation, unemployment, public spending, defence spending and industry under the Wave government? This article was in the *Lentz Times* a few days ago.

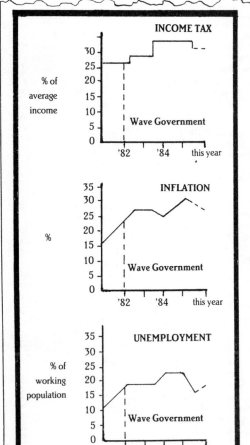

result of compromises in basic philosophy which brought it to power in 1982.

Nationalizations

In accordance with its original programme, the Wave government nationalized the fruit industry in 1983 and the clothing industry in 1984. Both industries were largely owned by foreign capital and, despite 60% compensation, the majority of our export markets were promptly closed in retaliation. The situation has eased a little since the government agreed to waive tax and minimum wage demands in the new electronics industries (70% foreign owned).

Public Spending

Social reform has been a central policy of the present government, but its success in this area has been partial.

The Wave government has increased subsidies to schools. These subsidies have been largely directed to rural areas where (according to government figures) they have helped to significantly reduce the illiteracy rate. There has also been some att

improving technical training, although 95% of our engineers are still trained abroad.

The government has also built eighteen hospitals, mostly in rural areas, thus reducing the ratio of one hospital per 40,000 population to one per 32,000.

The Wave government has built over 7,000 houses around the cities, but the programme has utterly failed to rehouse the slum populations as originally intended, and the houses have mainly gone to urban lower-middle classes instead, who can afford to pay the rent.

Defence Spending

The government has cut defence spending by 20%, but has continued to honour the contracts negotiated by the previous government. There has, accordingly, been no real reduction of power in the armed forces, as witnessed by the lack

The Sky party was in government from 1978 to 1982. What did it do about income tax? Did inflation go up? etc.

Ask your partner, and compare the two governments.

There will be an election next month. Discuss with your partner: What are the problems in Lentz at the moment? What should the new government do about public spending, etc.? Which party should be elected?

P ETER lives in Nigeria and works for a gas company. He plays the African drums very well, and he's taking evening classes in Spanish.

C AROL lives in Bristol. She's married and she teaches dance. At the moment, she's saving her money.

But how long have they been doing these things? Why did they start doing them?

Peter wrote this letter three years ago.

Carol wrote this one a few weeks ago.

Dear Penny,

As you can see, I've got a new address, and you'll probably want an explanation. Well, Carol and I got divorced about a year and a half ago. Soon after the divorce, Exel, the gas company, offered me a job in Nigeria, so I came to live here.

The job's perfect in a way, because I've always been interested in African music, and at last I've got the chance to play some. I've just started to learn how to play the African drums, and I think I've got talent!

Carol's still in Bristol. She got married again six months ago, and apparently she's very happy.

Much love,

Dear Penny,

Sorry I've been out of touch, but I've been quite busy recently. My baby, Samantha, had her first birthday last week. We had a small party for her, but I don't think she understood!

I'm working again. About three months ago I took a job teaching dance at a local school. I was so bored sitting at home all day! I'm trying to save some of my salary for Samantha's education, but it's <u>not</u> easy.

I still hear from Peter. He's leaving Nigeria next summer to work in Madrid, and he's only just started taking Spanish lessons!

Write back. I'd love to hear from you.

Love

Carol

Five years ago:

S UE lived in London. She worked in a restaurant and she was a little overweight. She wanted to get married.

J OHN lived in London and worked in a bank. He played a lot of sports in his free time, so he didn't smoke. He was single.

Your partner has got some recent information about them. Are they still the same? Do they still do the same things? If not, how long have they been different? Why did they change?

SUE lives in Manchester and works for a radio station there. She's slim and vegetarian.

JOHN's married and lives in London. He sometimes writes articles for a local newspaper, and he smokes too much.

But how long have they been doing these things?
Why did they start doing them?

Sue wrote this letter three years ago.

Dear Mike,

It was really nice to hear from you.

I'm fine. The only change recently is that there's a new girl sharing my flat with me. Her name's Alice and she's vegetarian. She's told me so many bad things about meat that I've decided to be vegetarian too, and I'm quite enjoying it! Speaking of food, did you know I went on a diet about a year ago? I'm so slim now you wouldn't recognise me!

I had a letter from John the other day. Did you know he had a car accident last year? He hurt his back, so he doesn't play any sports now, except swimming.

He's at the same London address, and wants you to write.

All love,

Sue—

John wrote this one a few weeks ago.

Dear Mike,

I'm not sure this is the right address, so I hope it reaches you.

The main news is that I got married about a year ago — and started smoking a few weeks later! We still have some arguments, but I <u>think</u> smoking makes me more patient....

I wrote my first sports article for the local newspaper last week. As you know, I can't play sports any more, so I decided to write about them — and the editor wants me to write another one.

Sue came to visit last week. She's still single, but happy about it now. She's got a job with a radio station in Manchester, and she's looking for a flat there. I quite envy her. I'm <u>still</u> at the bank!

yours
John

Five years ago:

CAROL and her husband, Peter, lived in Bristol. Peter worked in a car factory and Carol worked in a shop. Carol loved going out and spent a lot of money on new clothes. Peter was interested in music.

Your partner has got some recent information about them. Are they still the same? Do they still do the same things? If not, how long have they been different? Why did they change?

Work in a group with one or two other students.

1. Imagine the news stories for at least two of these photographs, and make notes. (Use the articles on pages 94 and 95 to help you with ideas for details.)

2. Your partner's group has been working on different news stories.

   Look at their photographs on page 96 and decide what you should ask them to find out about their stories. (Use the articles on pages 94 and 95 to help you with ideas for questions.)

3. Ask your partner's group your questions, and answer their questions about your stories.

   When you've finished, prepare a short radio news programme with all the news stories.

4. When each group has presented their news programmes, compare them.

   Did your partner's group miss any details in your stories? Did you miss any details in theirs?

The Nenebridge Reporter

ONLY 30P   YOUR DAILY PAPER

EXCLUSIVE

12 DIE IN M1 ACCIDENT

Twelve people died in an accident on the M1 motorway yesterday afternoon. The accident happened when a petrol lorry crashed into a safety barrier and exploded.

'It was raining heavily and there was a lot of traffic. The lorry was going quite fast – at about 65 mph – when a small car tried to move in front of it. The lorry just lost control, hit the barrier and exploded. It all happened so fast!' said Mr Calder, one of the people in the accident.

Twenty-seven people died or were seriously hurt in the accident. It took the police six hours to clear the motorway.

ITALY WINS 3-2

The match between England and Italy in Madrid last night was one of the most exciting games in the World Cup so far.

Both teams played extremely well, and the score was 2 – 2 until the last minutes of the second half. Then the Italian captain, Bernardo Rossi, scored a magnificent goal, making the final score Italy 3 England 2. It was Rossi's second goal of the match.

Other goal scorers were John Curtis and Sam Billing for England, and Marco Bertoli for Italy.

England will play Argentina next, and Italy will play Brazil.

Energy Bike

Dr Homes, an American, has invented a machine to save energy in the home. With it, you can get exercise, watch television and save money at the same time !

It's quite small – 15cm wide and 10cm deep – and it only weighs 800 grams. You can put it onto an ordinary exercise bicycle, plug in your TV or tape recorder, and start pedalling!

The machine will be on sale next March and will cost about £25.

70,000 SAY NO TO NUCLEAR ARMS

Seventy thousand people were in a demonstration in London yesterday against nuclear arms. They came from all over Britain and Europe to protest about both American and Soviet missiles in Europe.

The demonstration started in Hyde Park early this morning. From there it went to the American and Russian Embassies, and it finished in front of the Houses of Parliament.

It was well organized. There were only a few short fights between the police and the demonstrators, and there were no arrests.

There will be four more demonstrations around Great Britain this week, in Birmingham, Newcastle, Bristol and Edinburgh.

Children Trapped in Landslide

The police have rescued eight school children and their teacher from a cave in the Peak District, but three children are still trapped inside it.

The children and their teacher were visiting the cave yesterday when a landslide blocked the entrance. They were trapped for fourteen hours before the rescue team found them early this morning. No-one was badly hurt, but three of the children weren't with them.

'The three children have been in the cave for over twenty hours,' said Patrick Clark, the
(continued on column 3)

(continued from column 1)
leader of the rescue team, 'and we have to work very fast. The ground is still very wet and we think there will be another landslide.'

New Shopping Centre Planned

The City Council has decided to build a large shopping centre on the west side of Arlington Park in the city centre.

There will be a hypermarket, two department stores, over fifty small shops and four restaurants in the centre.

Work on the centre will start in March next year and it will take about two and a half years to build. The cost, at current prices, will be about ten million pounds.

There has been a lot of protest about the centre. David Barton, the chairman of the protest committee explained, 'Small shops in the area will lose their customers, and the people of Nenebridge will lose most of Arlington Park. We should improve the city centre of Nenebridge, not just add a shopping centre.'

Work in a group with one or two other students.

1. Imagine the news stories for at least two of these photographs, and make notes. (Use the articles on pages 94 and 95 to help you with ideas for details.)

2. Your partner's group has been working on different news stories.

   Look at their photographs on page 93 and decide what your should ask them to find out about their stories. (Use the articles on pages 94 and 95 to help you with ideas for questions.)

3. Ask your partner's group your questions, and answer their questions about your stories.

   When you've finished, prepare a short radio news programme with all the news stories.

4. When each group has presented their news programmes, compare them.

   Did your partner's group miss any details in your stories? Did you miss any details in theirs?

LOCAL NEWS

EXCLUSIVE REPORTS